"I have such deep admiration for the late Dr. Jerry Falwell and his wife, Macel. They labored tirelessly alongside each other for many years and, in doing so, nurtured a legacy that will endure for years to come. Only eternity will reveal the true extent of the lasting and far-reaching impact they've made."

—James Dobson, Focus on the Family

"Macel Falwell has accomplished many great things in life, raising a strong family and quietly supporting her husband. My friendship with Dr. Jerry Falwell was inspirational. I enjoyed visits on campus at Liberty University, watching Doc as he interacted with young people and admiring the respect they had for this great man who loved people—especially the younger generation. It was great fun to fellowship with Jerry and Macel—a woman who exemplified Proverbs 31. Jerry adored her and deeply respected her counsel. Reading her reflections about what God accomplished through their lives together is as thrilling as having watched it close-up. The stories are a blessing to all."

—Franklin Graham, president and CEO, Billy Graham Evangelistic Association and Samaritan's Purse

"Dr. Jerry Falwell was the same in public and in private. His extraordinary love of people, deep biblical convictions, and visionary drive combined to make him one of our nation's most influential figures. He never lost sight that it was about Jesus—not about him."

—Mike Huckabee, former governor of Arkansas

"Jerry Falwell was a man of courage. A servant leader of God, he lived his faith without hesitation or fear. Not once did he consider lighting a lamp and hiding it under a bushel. No: he placed his lamp upon a stand, where it gave light to the whole house. A man of deep wisdom, Dr. Falwell understood something quite profound, something that too many people today would rather not acknowledge. What he understood was the deep resonance between the demands of his faith and the demands of his nation. He saw that as the Bible requires Christians to bear witness to the truth, so too does the Declaration of Independence require Americans to bear witness to certain self-evident truths. Jerry once said that his heart 'was burning to serve Christ' and that because of it 'nothing would ever be the same.' It was true. Because of his heart and because of his courage, America is not the same. Jerry Falwell understood that the relentless efforts to drive God from American public life would inevitably affect our respect for life itself. It would pressure believers to hide their lamps beneath a bushel. Jerry refused. He would not be passive. He would not be ashamed. He would not be cowed. Instead, he would bear witness. And he would act on those convictions."

—Newt Gingrich, former member, U.S. House of Repesentatives

"I know what some say about the public figure, the man of controversy and conflict. What matters to me is what I know about the private man. He was a good man whose goal in life was to serve his master by showing compassion to those in need, providing comfort to those in pain, and, most important of all, sharing the blessings of life eternal by preaching his faith in the risen Lord. To hear him talk with such evident passion about his God, his family, his church, and the university he created was to know the true spirit of a person moved by the love of Christ."

—Karl Rove, former adviser to President George W. Bush

"One of the joys of my life was to have Jerry Falwell as a friend. He was a faithful soldier for Christ, a happy Christian, and a tremendous family man. His wife, Macel, shares her life with this giant of the faith. You will be blessed."

—Jerry Vines, founder, Jerry Vines Ministries

"I miss Jerry. I miss his enthusiasm. I miss his down-to-earth preaching. I miss his leadership among faith-based believers. But, most of all, I miss his friendship. Thankfully, his legacy will live on through his family and the God-ordained institutions he founded. I don't think I have ever met another man quite like Jerry Falwell."

—H. B. London, vice president, Focus on the Family

JERRY FALWELL

His Life and Legacy

Macel Falwell

with Melanie Hemry

HOWARD BOOKS
A DIVISION OF SIMON & SCHUSTER

NEW YORK   LONDON   TORONTO   SYDNEY

Our purpose at Howard Books is to:
- *Increase faith* in the hearts of growing Christians
- *Inspire holiness* in the lives of believers
- *Instill hope* in the hearts of struggling people everywhere

Because He's coming again!

Published by Howard Books, a division of Simon & Schuster, Inc.
1230 Avenue of the Americas, New York, NY 10020
HOWARD www.howardpublishing.com
BOOKS

Jerry Falwell: His Life and Legacy © 2008 by Macel Falwell

In association with Jeff Dunn at the literary agency of
Winters, King & Associates, Inc., Tulsa, Oklahoma

Library of Congress Cataloging-in-Publication Data

Falwell, Macel.
    Jerry Falwell : his life and legacy / Macel Falwell.
        p.   cm.
    1.   Falwell, Jerry. 2. Baptists—United States—Clergy—Biography. I. Title.
BX6495.F3F35   2008
286'.1092—dc22   2008006461
[B]

ISBN-13: 978-1-4165-8028-7
ISBN-10:   1-4165-8028-X
10 9 8 7 6 5 4 3 2 1

Manufactured in the United States of America

For information regarding special discounts for bulk purchases,
please contact: Simon & Schuster Special Sales at
1-800-456-6798 or business@simonandschuster.com.

Edited by Jeff Gerke
Cover design by Stephanie D. Walker
Interior design by Jaime Putorti

"Larry Flynt: My Friend, Jerry Falwell" reprinted courtesy of Larry Flynt.

Scripture quotations marked NKJV are taken from the *New King James Version*®.
Copyright © 1982 by Thomas Nelson, Inc. Used by permission. All rights reserved.
Scripture quotations marked NIV are taken from the *Holy Bible, New International
Version*®. Copyright © 1973, 1978, 1984 by International Bible Society. Used by
permission of Zondervan. All rights reserved.

1933 Jerry and Gene Falwell born, August 11
Macel Pate born, October 4

1952 Jerry born again at Park Avenue Baptist Church,
January 20

1956 Jerry graduates from Baptist Bible College in Springfield, Missouri

Founds Thomas Road Baptist Church

Starts daily radio broadcast

Starts television ministry

1958 Jerry and Macel married, April 12

1962 Jerry Falwell Jr. born, June 17

1964 Jean Ann "Jeannie" Falwell born, November 7

1966 Jonathan Falwell born, September 7

1971 Jerry founds Lynchburg Baptist College (later Liberty
University)

1973   SEC charges filed against Thomas Road Baptist
Church, July 3

Thomas Road Baptist Church cleared of charges,
August 10

1979   Jerry forms the Moral Majority

1983   Jerry sues *Hustler* magazine for libel; the case is battled
in court through 1988

1987   Jim Bakker asks Jerry to take over the failing PTL
Club

1997   Following Jerry's two forty-day fasts, Liberty University receives a $52 million miracle

2001   Virginia State Council of Education approves Liberty
University's Ph.D. program

2003   David Green, owner of Hobby Lobby, purchases
Ericsson plant for Thomas Road Baptist Church

2004   Liberty University moves into renovated property debt
free

2005   Jerry suffers respiratory arrest twice and has to be
resuscitated

2006   Thomas Road Baptist Church celebrates fiftieth
anniversary in new sanctuary

2007   Jerry Falwell goes home to be with the Lord, May 15

This book is dedicated to my loving husband, Jerry. He was the greatest husband that I could have ever asked for, and he proved that each and every day. He inspired me in ways I never would have thought possible. And that inspiration lives on in so many of us who loved him.

I also dedicate this book to Jerry Jr., Jeannie, and Jonathan. Their love has always sustained me, now more than ever. Also, to Becki and Shari, who have been amazing spouses for my sons.

Last, I want to dedicate this book to my grandchildren, Trey, Wesley, Jonathan Jr., Jessica, Paul, Natalie, Nicholas, and Caroline. You bring me joy in unspeakable ways. Jerry's spirit lives on in all of you.

CONTENTS

ACKNOWLEDGMENTS

I would like to say a special word of thanks to Melanie Hemry who helped make this book a reality. To say that I couldn't have done this without you would be an understatement.

I would also like to say thanks to Tom Winters and Jeff Dunn, who worked tirelessly to ensure that the story of my life with Jerry would be told. To Denny Boultinghouse and the entire Howard team . . . thank you for believing in this story and encouraging me to write it. Thank you all for your efforts.

Thanks to my three wonderful children for doing so much to help me during the most difficult time of my life. I know your love has sustained me in ways I will never fully understand.

I would like to say a special word of thanks to my wonderful daughters-in-law. While Jerry, Jeannie, and Jonathan have done so much to take care of me, Becki and Shari have been amazing, as well. They have done so much to help me through this time. For allowing the grandchildren to stay with me so often, for taking me to more restaurants than I can remember, and for everything else . . . thanks!

Thanks to the eight most wonderful grandchildren in the

world. Thanks for all of the slumber parties and trips to the toy store. I couldn't have asked for better grandchildren than you.

To my sister Jean, and her husband, Eugene, thank you for the countless hours you have spent in helping me after Jerry's death. To my brother, Sonny, and his wife, Carole, thank you for always being there for me. You are all very special. To all of my family, you have been so wonderful to me and you continue to make life an amazing experience.

To my church family at Thomas Road Baptist Church: Words cannot express my appreciation for the outpouring of love and support you have shown me. All of you are a perfect example of what the New Testament church should be. Thank you.

I would also like to express my deepest appreciation for all of you who agreed to be interviewed for this book, and for each of you who have been armor bearers standing alongside Jerry and me and our family over the years. Although you are too numerous to mention individually, you know who you are, I know who you are, and God knows who you are. Thank you for your love, prayers, and support.

A.W. Tozer, the great twentieth-century theologian, prolific author, and preacher, had it exactly right when he acknowledged his reason for writing the beloved Christian standard *The Pursuit of God*.

"The only book that should ever be written," Tozer observed, "is one that flows up from the heart, forced out by the inward pressure. When such a work has gestated within a man it is almost certain that it will be written. The man who is thus charged with a message will not be turned back by any blasé consideration. His book will be to him not only imperative, it will be inevitable."

And Tozer wrote that more than five decades ago! Imagine what he might say today, when anyone—indeed, *everyone*—seems able to crank out a book the very instant a catchy phrase or two comes to mind. Ours has become a nation in which the contents of most bestselling books amount to little more than overhyped stacks of partisan political swipes, self-indulgent autobiographies, mindless how-to guides, and, worst of all, soulless attacks against the very existence of our Creator.

The book you hold here, though, will neither be defined nor measured by any industry or wordly standard. In fact, this book is one of those "imperatives" Tozer must have been talking about. Here, Macel Falwell has blessed us with a refreshingly simple, honest, and deeply felt labor of love that invites us in to her well-lived marriage of forty-nine years to Dr. Jerry Falwell, who, all too soon at age seventy-two, entered into his glory on May 15, 2007. And in our reading it, you will soon find, we are ultimately called to a higher standard as both Christians and Americans.

In humility, innocence, and an endearing gentleness of spirit, Macel shares with us a man, a marriage, and a family, all fundamentally united and ordered on faith in God, a commitment to His service and to one another. But even deeper yet, somewhere in the essence of Macel's written words, she unwittingly reveals the converging components of the pure Dr. Falwell—both in his private relationships and in his public ministries—which begin to meld into a template for us of what it looks like to live, today, by faith. In reading this, we would all do well to look upon and follow Dr. Falwell's matchless example of how to step out and stand for God's truth, no matter the challenges or consequences.

Indeed, in Dr. Falwell we found a unique and tremendous supernatural visionary—a great warrior—in growing God's kingdom on earth. And atop each of God's victories through him, Macel superimposes the heart of her dear husband as only she could: we find here a doting father, a compassionate pastor, staunch patriot, a serial practical joker—and a friend in all seasons for all people. From Dr. Falwell's rough-and-tumble boyhood days in Lynchburg to the meteoric rise of Thomas Road Baptist Church, the Moral Majority, and his beloved Liberty University, Macel shows us a Jerry Falwell who was just as much a foot soldier for his family and for the body of Christ as he was, in his public life, a mighty leader in this country for the Lord.

We came to know Dr. Falwell as a man of God who commanded meetings and held counsel with American presidents and international dignitaries. We watched as he built a congregation with thirty-five members into the eighth-largest church in the country. He turned his vision for a college into the number one evangelical university in the nation. He imploded and reshaped the American political landscape by rallying millions of Christians into the most powerful values-based voting bloc in the history of this country to date. And he took the gospel of Jesus Christ, first on foot through the neighborhoods of Lynchburg, then on to television, to radio, and finally, across the world, winning souls and pioneering missions all in the name of, and in the glory of, God.

But Macel also shows us the private Falwell, the family man, the sense of humor, the big happy kid, just as clearly. She describes how she constantly, yet lovingly, had to admonish her husband for giving away the very shoes on his feet, his coats, and all the money he had in his pockets (or in his bank account!) to someone he met who was in need. Throughout their marriage, at the first hint of a rainstorm, Dr. Falwell would politely get up and excuse himself from whatever meeting he happened to be in at the time and run home to be with Macel, who's always been afraid of thunder and lightning! In fact, Macel tells so many warm and funny stories about their newlywed years, their family holidays and vacations (and her cooking!), that it eventually becomes natural to chuckle over something she's shared with us even after we've put the book down. Macel's tribute here makes it difficult—nearly impossible—not to find a whole new way to love the Jerry Falwell we already knew.

Of course, Dr. Falwell had his critics throughout his career—who in the public eye doesn't? But he expected such challenges and, in prayer and by faith, refused to be deterred. Macel tells us Dr. Falwell never minded being made a "fool" of for the gospel—and we are all the better for it. Along with the rest of the country, Dr. Falwell grappled with and prayed over the unfolding controversial issues of his time—politics, poverty, human rights, and civil rights. Yet, from beginning to end, Dr. Falwell had the truth with him and put it to use in everything he said and did.

Macel makes it very plain for us here: next to God, Jerry Falwell was at the core, the absolute heart, of the Falwell family and all those who surrounded him. But what's truly best about Macel—as she pours out this tribute to her husband and to his body of work—is that she manages to make that clear to us without really trying.

They say that behind every great man is a great woman. True as it is, even that is much too trite for what we learn from these two people. While Macel chose to stay home and grow the Falwell family in the roots of traditional biblical values and faith, she was never *behind* her husband by any means. She was, in fact, at his side—supporting, encouraging, counseling, tempering, and doing a lot of laughing. This self-described shy church pianist and her larger-than-life preacher may have been polar opposites, as Macel describes for us, but they were partners in Christ.

That, after all, is the legacy this book has to leave us with. Even before reading Macel's heartened words, we already knew, admired, and respected Jerry Falwell for his work in building lives, churches, ministries, and a university from which thousands of students he called champions for Christ go every day into the world for all kinds of God's glory in service. We already knew that Dr. Falwell dramatically and positively changed the way Christians long thought of themselves and the influence, as the body of Christ, they commanded in the last three decades amid the gathering darkness of our society. And by God's hand on Dr. Falwell, we all became inspired by his hard-won vision for all believers to go out, beyond the four walls of our sanctuaries, and make a concrete difference in the world in the name of God.

Indeed, to have Macel now compile all of her husband's memories, victories, and challenges like this into one whole cloth leaves us with a rather stunning testament to his legacy here on earth. But, again, the legacy of Jerry Falwell abides just as brightly in the all too rare picture Macel gives us of their strong and steadfast marriage and their family, all of it nurtured and anchored in Christ. In fact, three of the most vital living pillars of Dr. Falwell's legacy do not go unnoticed in their mother's effort here: Jerry Falwell Jr., now chancellor of Liberty University; Jonathan, senior pastor at Thomas Road Baptist Church; and Jeannie, a surgeon, all of whom are serving and glorifying Jesus today in the tradition of their beloved father, absolutely—but with their distinctively *own* hands and feet.

Macel Falwell has given us, really, an invaluable gift in this piece of history. Hers is a work that selflessly shines divine light on the soul of one of the world's truest champions for Christ. At the same time, Jerry Falwell's life becomes for us an immeasurable footprint of God's work in the world. And we need that now. We should turn to Dr. Falwell's life and his legacy as something faithful we can to refer to in these throw-away, here-today-gone-tomorrow times of instant gratification and pervasive godlessness. We need something to go back to and ponder over when we're looking for someone to measure ourselves against, to hold ourselves accountable and to occasionally ask ourselves, "Are we doing enough as Christians?" Some of us will treasure Dr. Falwell's memories on these pages when we simply need something to smile about.

There is no doubt that this message is exactly the kind A. W. Tozer once described as a book that had to be written. This story has been gestating in Macel, for much of the last fifty years, flowing up from the heart of this wife, this mother, and this partner and champion for Christ in so many ways in her own right. We are grateful that her writing was, truly and divinely, inevitable.

CHAPTER ONE

Jesus, Jerry, and Me

I t was a warm spring evening in Lynchburg, Virginia. Monday, May 14, 2007. My husband, Jerry Falwell, and I drove across town enjoying how the Blue Ridge Mountains stood in timeless majesty against an azure sky, dressed in verdant green trees. Their branches waved in the gentle breeze like a benediction.

"Would you like to go to O'Charley's for dinner?" Jerry said, the usual twinkle of good humor in his eyes. "It's Monday."

"Oh Jerry, I'd forgotten!"

On Monday nights O'Charley's offered steak soup, a new dish on the menu. I'd longed to try it again, but I seemed to think of it only on Wednesday or Thursday or Saturday. Most people wouldn't expect a man like Jerry Falwell, who had so many major issues on his mind, to remember a little thing like getting his wife a bowl of steak soup. But then, most people didn't know my husband.

The crowd at O'Charley's was light as we slid into a booth. Jerry nodded and waved at some people across the room. We'd never met the young woman who waited on us, but after forty-nine years of marriage, I wasn't surprised by my husband's kindness to her.

"Where do you go to college?" he asked.

"I go to the community college," she said with a shy smile.

"Why aren't you at my university?" Jerry asked. "Liberty University."

"My parents can't afford it," she said, shrugging one shoulder.

"If you'd like to go to Liberty, I'll give you a full scholarship."

Her eyes lit like sparklers on the Fourth of July. "Are you *serious?*"

Jerry assured her that he was serious, and she floated away in a haze of disbelief. She'd had no idea when she walked up to our booth with her pad in hand that her life was about to change forever. But after almost fifty years of marriage to Jerry, I could have predicted it.

Once, some children had knocked a baseball over the fence into our yard. Before giving the ball back to them, Jerry wrote a message on it promising a scholarship at Liberty, and then he signed it. "Wait!" he yelled, chasing the kids down the street. "I want to add that it's a four-year scholarship." So I smiled at the young waitress who tried to be sedate but almost jumped for joy as she walked away.

Something else stands out in my mind about that evening. I remember that Jerry ate no more than two or three bites of his food. Instead, he seemed content to gaze across the table, his eyes tracing the familiar features of my face in a most unusual way.

It was almost as though he was seeing me for the first time. Or the last. As soon as the thought formed I pushed it aside. Jerry had looked across the table at me for almost fifty years.

Still . . . he focused on my face.

I savored my soup, aware of his scrutiny. Young people like our waitress often think those of our generation are trite when we repeat such worn expressions as, "Where did all the years go?" But one day they, like the rest of us, will look up, stunned that fifty years could have been so . . . *brief*.

That's why, as Jerry watched emotions flicker across my face, I reflected over our life together, and marveled. It had been quite a ride—not at all what I'd envisioned when I'd married the skinny young man who founded Thomas Road Baptist Church.

Back then, neither of us had any idea where our journey would take us. I, for one, am glad. Timid as I've always been, it is best that I did not foresee meetings in the White House, traveling around the world, protestors, death threats, bomb threats, and a kidnapping plot. God's plan for our lives is so much bigger than anything we can imagine, and though I would have shied away from it had I known what lay ahead, I'm so grateful I did not miss it.

Neither Jerry nor I imagined that God was forging us into instruments He would use to affect thousands of people and the politics of a nation. We were unaware of the tapestry He'd been weaving all along. We just thought we were living our lives.

That's the way God works, but we didn't know that then.

Polar Opposites

I don't think what makes our story relevant is Jerry or Macel Falwell. We were . . . how shall I say it? . . . unlikely candidates. You could search the world and have trouble finding two more opposite people than Jerry and me.

I was a prim and proper lady who'd been raised in the arms of a hardworking, protective Christian family. Jerry used to say that, in my family, failing to pay a tithe was akin to murder. Though it was a bit of an exaggeration, he had a point.

In my home on Christmas morning, no one unwrapped a gift until the Christmas story had been read from the book of Luke. We never listened to any music except Christian music. We did not watch movies, and alcohol was forbidden. I was the youngest of three daughters with a younger brother on whom we doted. I was timid and hesitant about life, a trait that would progress with the years.

Jerry was the son of a bootlegger. His father was an agnostic and his grandfather an avowed atheist. His father shot and killed his own brother in self-defense. He was a shrewd businessman who made a small fortune, while drinking himself to death.

Jerry and his twin brother, Gene, were the youngest of five children in the Falwell family. Their mother, a quiet Christian woman, was a saint in the midst of a rough and rowdy family of Southern rebels.

I spent my younger years committed to Christ and to His church. Jerry had grown up without such commitment. Over the years his mother pressed him to go to church. For a while he accommodated her, but most Sundays Jerry walked in the front door and slipped out the back when no one was looking.

Throughout our marriage I was shy, fearful, and ever certain that none of Jerry's wild ideas would work. Jerry believed that *anything* was possible through prayer and hard work.

So you see, our story is not relevant because of who we were, for we were polar opposites, ordinary people with ordinary weaknesses, whose lives intersected with Jesus. Our story is relevant only because it reveals what God can do with two ordinary, if unlikely, people who dare to say yes to Him.

The Bible says that the foolishness of God is wiser than men, and the weakness of God is stronger than men (1 Corinthians 1:25). Somehow, Jesus took us—weak, foolish vessels that we were—and confounded the wisdom of the world.

Our story is about Jerry, Jesus, and me, and what happened when our lives intersected.

In the Beginning

Jerry continued to gaze at my face while I ate my soup and pondered our differences. Why I was the one who had ended up sharing his life, I'll never know. *I* wasn't a fearless defender of human rights, after all. I felt ill-suited for life in the limelight. But strange as it might seem, I was the one God and Jerry chose. I guess they saw something in me—the skittish little girl born on October 4, 1933, to Sam and Lucie Pate—that I didn't.

What was it? Perhaps in part it was the heritage of faith, love, and integrity that I received from my parents. My father, Sam Pate, had been raised in a Christian home in Alum Creek, West Virginia. Although he was one of the smartest men I've ever known, Daddy completed school only through the third grade. Back in those days, you could teach school if you finished fifth. A lean man with brown hair and warm eyes, he moved to Richmond, Virginia, at the age of eighteen and found work.

A coworker invited him home for the weekend and Daddy met—and lost his heart to—a pretty young woman he saw sitting on the front step of the house next door. Her name was Lucile Donald and, of course, she became my mother.

A Supernatural Intersection

I was twelve years old when I gave my heart to Jesus. Six years later, still riding the wave of His love, I was swept into my first encounter with the man who would forever change my life. The stage for our meeting was set when the little Baptist church we attended sent a few families, including ours, to plant a new church—Park Avenue Baptist. The new church had a cheery wooden sanctuary and two pianos, one on either side of the platform. My friend Delores Clark played one piano and I played the other. We also played for the pastor's early-morning radio broadcast.

During those years, I did not lack for male attention. But my pastor's young brother-in-law, Julius, was the most persistent. A handsome young man, he was pursuing a career as minister of music. Although my parents were very strict about my relationships, my mother adored Julius, and I was flattered when he proposed to me. The truth is that I was more interested in the concept of marriage than in its reality. When Julius slipped an engagement ring on my finger, I knew I wasn't ready to leave my happy family to make one of my own.

I don't want to hurt his feelings, I thought. *I can always give it back to him later.*

I didn't mind being engaged, but I had no interest in getting married.

One Sunday night in January 1952, wearing my sparkling engagement ring, I dressed for church in a black velveteen dress with white trim. The sanctuary, which held three hundred people, was filled almost to capacity. Delores and I were playing hymns when ushers brought three teenage boys to seats in the front. I noticed that one of them in particular, although skinny, was quite handsome.

His name was Jerry Falwell.

The Man Behind the Media Image

O'Charley's had begun to fill with the evening crowd and I stopped eating my soup long enough to say hello as friends and acquaintances passed by. Still watching my face, Jerry leaned against the padded booth, looking for all the world like he, too, was remembering the first time he saw me back in 1952.

Our waitress brought hot rolls baked a deep golden brown just the way I liked them. As I buttered my bread, I paused to study *his* face. The thing that still amazed me after all these years was how many of the media portrayals had painted a bizarre public persona of Jerry that most of the world believed to be true. Some said he was a

> *If I was the polar opposite of Jerry, he was the polar opposite of his public persona.*
> —MACEL FALWELL

7

hatemonger, stern, humorless, rigid, and uncompromising. I smiled just thinking about it. All you had to do was look at the laugh lines etched in his face to know at least part of that perception was wrong.

If I was the polar opposite of Jerry, *he* was the polar opposite of his public persona.

The Falwell family traced its roots in Virginia to the early 1600s, and those roots were anything but straitlaced and puritanical. Jerry's great-great grandfather, Hezekiah Carey Falwell, and his brother John arrived in Lynchburg in 1850. In 1914, Jerry's grandmother, Martha Catherine Bell Falwell, died from a crippling disease. The moment Martha drew her last breath, Jerry's grandfather turned his back on God.

Their son Carey grew up to be an avowed agnostic. In 1910, he courted Helen Beasley, driving a smart black horse-drawn buggy. They married August 7, 1918; Carey was twenty-two and Helen was twenty.

> *Dad got his love of people from his mother. She was a saint.*
> —JERRY FALWELL JR.

Helen was one of the only signs of spiritual life on Jerry's family tree. She'd grown up one of sixteen children raised in a devout Baptist home in the small town of Hollywood, Virginia. Her family didn't have much money, but every Sunday morning all eighteen of them worshipped at the Hollywood Baptist Church. Helen, who stood five feet eight inches tall, wore her waist-length auburn hair braided and wrapped in a bun. In addition to the apron she always wore in the kitchen, Helen rose every morning with a smile that never left her face.

Helen was a quiet woman with incredible faith in God. In the eighty-two years of her life, no one ever saw her angry. Even the discipline she meted out to her young children was offered in love. Her unfailing faith and unflagging good humor were two traits she passed down to Jerry.

Carey and Helen lived on a farm on Rustburg Road. The two-story white house was home for them and their five children. Their oldest daughter, Virginia, was born in 1917. Their second daughter, Rosha, was born in 1921. Their first son, Lewis, was born in 1924. Rosha died of a ruptured appendix when she was only ten. Two years later, on August 11, 1933, Helen gave birth to twin sons, Jerry and Gene.

The Money Myth

Our waitress at O'Charley's, still awash with amazement over the scholarship Jerry had offered her, hovered at our table for a moment to see if there was anything else we needed. Jerry still hadn't touched his food, nor had he taken his eyes off me except when speaking to someone else.

How many people in America would be as stunned as our waitress at Jerry's generosity? Probably the majority, because part of the public's misconception about Jerry had to do with money. After the PTL scandal in the eighties, many people believed that all televangelists were motivated by money. That wasn't true. Jerry's weakness with money was not a tendency to hoard it, but to give it all away. At one time Liberty University was in financial trouble, in part because Jerry had given so many full scholarships to young people he wanted to help that there weren't enough students paying tuition.

Money was nothing more than a tool for Jerry, largely because it had been nothing more than a tool for his father, Carey. Though Carey was an uneducated man, he had an uncanny ability to create wealth. He was a visionary who could look at the world around him, see what services would be required, and offer them. He owned bus lines, real estate, stocks and bonds, and gas stations across sixteen counties. He distributed oil and gas for Standard, Shell, Texaco, and Quaker Oil. He bought land, rental property, restaurants, and an inn. One of his more infamous roles in Lynchburg was buying and selling bootleg liquor. In 1935, he built the Merry Garden Dance Hall and Dining Room, which overlooked Lynchburg. That is by no means a complete list of his business ventures.

Enjoying the fruits of his labors, Carey rode to work in a chauffeur-driven car and had at least six men working on the farm at all times. He hired help for Helen in the kitchen. Jerry and Gene had a full-time nanny, a black man named David Brown, whom they loved. While Carey enjoyed making money, money never owned him. He used his wealth to make his family more comfortable and to help those in need. As often as not he let homeless people or those down on their luck live in the rental property he owned and the houses that dotted his property.

He used to leave piles of cash on the table, and when Jerry found out that one of his friends was from a poor family, Carey let the child help himself to the money. Because money was always plentiful, it meant very little to Jerry. He never suffered from lack. Because his own father had provided for him so well, when Jerry became a Christian he never doubted that his heavenly Father would do the same.

Live Bait for Sale

Of course, Jerry coupled his faith in God's goodness with an equal measure of hard work. He learned his work ethic when he was young and it did not change as he matured.

Carey was the one who taught him. He understood his sons' mischievous streak and decided early on that the best way to keep them out of trouble was to keep them busy. When Jerry and Gene were eleven, Carey came up with a business idea for them. First, he took the boys to large creeks and taught them how to seine for minnows and use a net to catch them. Then he taught them how to divide the catch into various sizes and showed the boys how to transport their catch to the little creek that ran in front of their house to await fishermen. Finally, he helped them make a sign: Live Minnows for Bait.

Fishermen often called ahead and placed their orders, and the twins took turns filling them each night. Around two in the morning the fishermen would pull up out front and honk. Either Gene or Jerry would hustle down and exchange bait for money. Often in the wee hours of the morning, the boys would look up and see Carey watching from his upstairs bedroom window, a wide smile on his face.

At first, Carey sent a car and driver with Gene and Jerry to seine for minnows, but in time he just lent them a truck and sent them on their way. He taught them to drive while they were in elementary school, and by age twelve they were racing around the farm on their own motorbikes. When they turned thirteen, Carey took them to the armory in town and got them their driver's licenses (he actually lied, saying they were fifteen). From April through October for the next several years, Gene and Jerry sold live bait, making $150 to $200 a week—an enormous amount of money for kids in the 1940s.

The Honest Truth

Not only did Jerry's generosity defy the popular misconceptions about televangelists, he broke the mold in other ways too. Some of Jerry's critics assumed that any preacher who held up a high moral standard in public must be hiding private sin. They accused him of being hypocritical and dishonest. He was neither.

Honest to a fault, when angry protestors at Harvard University asked Jerry if he was a racist, he replied, "I once was." The ugly stain of racism was woven into the fabric of everyday life in the South and, like most southerners, Jerry had to wrestle to get free of it. He refused to pretend that racism had never reared its ugly head in his life.

The honesty that marked him as a man had its roots in the farmhouse on Rustburg Road. There Jerry's mother and father managed somehow to create an atmosphere of love and acceptance that made him secure enough to tell the truth even when he knew he would pay a price for it.

In spite of the family's challenges, theirs was a happy home filled with laughter. Gene and Jerry spent carefree days playing tag, digging forts, and climbing apple trees. They fed chickens and hogs, chopped firewood, and looked forward to the end of Carey's workday, when he would spend time with them while Helen and their older sister, Virginia, made dinner. Carey got them a little cart with harnesses that allowed goats to pull them around the farm. For pets they had ponies, horses, and goats.

The Truth Will Set You Free

When Gene and Jerry went to first grade together at Mountain View Elementary School, the character (and mischief) that had been instilled in them during those early years began to emerge. After one year, Jerry was advanced to third grade, skipping second. Jerry always said it was because the school principal didn't think any teacher should have to endure both Falwell twins in the same class.

Jerry's third-grade teacher, Ida Clair Garbee, soon found it necessary to give him a well-deserved spanking. Years later, when asked why she paddled Jerry, she laughed. "Because he was a mischievous little buzzard! But one thing I liked about Jerry Falwell: he always told the truth. If he did something wrong, he admitted it. If Jerry said he didn't do something, he didn't do it." That kind of personal honesty was a trait that marked Jerry's life.

Apparently that honesty continued to impress Mrs. Garbee's family as her niece, Rebecca, whom Jerry called Old Grey Fox and her husband, Gordon, later became charter members of Thomas Road Baptist Church, and are still active members today. Gordon is the church's oldest living original deacon.

A Merry Heart

Just as Jerry's honesty endured and grew throughout his life, so did his love of laughter and good-hearted mischief. Jerry inherited from his father not only his visionary abilities but also Carey's talent and appreciation for practical jokes.

That became evident when Jerry was still a youngster. Once when his friend William was scheduled to visit, Jerry asked his father to think of a joke to pull on him. When William walked into the warm farmhouse, smelling the perpetual aromas of delicious food that Helen prepared, the Falwell boys launched their prank. William followed the mouthwatering scent into the kitchen, whereupon Carey shouted, *"Don't move!"*

To both William's and Jerry's stunned surprise, Carey whipped out a gun, and shot a hole in the floor just inches from William's feet. Eyes the size of dinner plates, William stood frozen with fear as Carey blew the smoke from the barrel of his gun. "I've been trying to get that fly all day."

William never came back.

During Jerry's years at Brookville High School, he may have set a world record for the number of practical jokes played by one student. On one occasion, he locked his gym teacher in the storage area and pinned his pants to the bulletin board. Another time Jerry arrived at math class only to discover that his teacher was giving them a test that day. He announced that he wasn't in the mood for a test, locked the teacher in her closet, and dismissed class.

One of his more famous escapades involved a teacher named Mrs. Cox. Mrs. Cox kept a stash of cookies in the drawer of her desk. While the class copied questions from the blackboard, she slipped one hand into the drawer for a cookie. Looking down, she covered her mouth with her hand and chewed, feeling certain that no one knew what she was doing.

The truth was that the whole class watched, mesmerized by the delectable morsels. Finally, Jerry decided to get even. He brought a live rat to school in a burlap bag. Before class, he put the rat in the drawer with the cookies.

"Now, I want you to turn in your books to page number . . . ," Mrs. Cox said as she inched the drawer open.

Without warning, the rat sprang from the drawer and landed in her lap. A look of horror crossed Mrs. Cox's face as she leapt from her chair, screamed, and fell into a dead faint.

The Wall Gang

During those years, Lynchburg youth separated themselves into neighborhood gangs. Although most of the rivalry took place on the playing field during sports season, at other times the gangs found different ways to keep busy. Jerry was a member of the Fairview Heights gang, a group of up to forty neighborhood kids who hung out on a low cement wall across the street from the Pickeral Café. Nicknamed the Wall Gang, they controlled who crossed the nearby bridge.

Because Jerry was the only member of the Wall Gang with a car—he drove a 1934 Plymouth—he became the leader of the pack. Somehow they got their hands on a mannequin, which they dressed and smeared with animal blood. On dark nights they left the bloody mannequin in the middle of the street. From their hiding place, they would watch horrified drivers turn the corner and hit the mannequin, believing it to be a human.

Inevitably, such pranks backfire on the pranksters themselves, and Jerry's case was no exception. In fact, Jerry would have given the valedictorian speech for his class if one of his pranks hadn't come home to roost.

During his junior and senior years, Jerry was captain of the football team. He discovered that the father of one of the boys on the team had donated the safe that housed the meal tickets for the cafeteria. Jerry talked the boy into finding out the combination. For two years the whole football team ate free on the tickets that Jerry distributed to them.

His senior year, someone finally noticed the discrepancy between the tickets sold and the money collected. For the first time, Jerry faced serious consequences for one of his pranks. His mother paid back the money for his lunch tickets, but the principal said, "Jerry, you will not give the valedictorian address."

Jerry smiled and acted cavalier, but inside he ached with humiliation. He'd worked hard to earn the role of valedictorian and was crushed to have lost the opportunity. He was an excellent athlete. He'd played baseball, basketball, and football. He was captain of the football team, class president, and a reporter for and later the editor of the school newspaper, *The Brookville Bee*. He graduated from high school at the age of sixteen, but he did not give his valedictorian address.

Thirty years later the school had mercy on him. He was asked to come back to the high school and give his speech at last. His topic for that speech: the consequences of one's actions.

The God of Second Chances

Maybe experiences like that were part of the reason Jerry offered so much mercy and forgiveness to everyone over the years. He identified with secretaries who made mistakes, rebellious students who broke the rules, and adults caught in the snares of sin. He'd once been a young man who turned his back on the Lord and broke the rules. He believed in a God of second and third and fourth chances.

Maybe Jerry never gave up on anyone because his mother, the faithful Helen Falwell, never gave up on him.

During his childhood, Helen took Jerry and his brother Gene with her to the Franklin Street Baptist Church Sunday after Sunday, despite the fact that as soon as possible they darted out the back door and ran down the street to their uncle Matthew Ferguson's house. Matthew, a nonbeliever, watched for the boys and had the door open for them when they arrived. While Helen thought they were in Sunday school, they were actually eating sweet rolls, drinking orange juice, and reading the cartoons in the Sunday paper.

By the time he was a teenager, Jerry stopped going to church altogether, and Carey refused to support Helen's efforts to get him there. However, Helen prayed—and the Holy Spirit gave her great wisdom. Every Sunday morning when Jerry wanted nothing more than to sleep in, she made sure the aroma of his favorite foods filled the house. In addition, she tuned the radio to the *Old Fashioned Revival Hour* and turned it up loud enough that he *couldn't* sleep. Week after week, he heard Rudy Atwood playing the piano and Dr. Charles Fuller preaching over the airwaves.

Jerry never lost the awareness that without his mother's prayers his life would have had a far different outcome. Because neither his mother nor God ever gave up on him, he never gave up on other people.

The Turning Point

He never hated people, either. *Hatemonger* was the ugliest term Jerry's enemies ever pinned on him. Jerry never hated anyone or anything in his life, except sin and Satan. He had the ability to hate a particular sin but love the sinner. For instance, he never minced words about what he thought about pornography. He sued Larry Flynt and *Hustler* magazine for dragging his deceased mother into their filthy innuendos. Even though they battled all the way to the Supreme Court, Jerry nevertheless *liked* Larry Flynt. Those two men—different in almost every way—were friends.

Jerry Falwell and Ted Kennedy were on opposite ends of every political issue, but in the media they were labeled the Odd Couple. The oddity was that the two men liked and respected one another.

Jerry loved people. He collected lifelong friends. And once his enemies met him, they joined the ranks. Truth be told, Jerry's circle of friends had been expanding since he was a kid. His mother learned to accommodate their growing number early on.

Gene and Jerry's bedroom had a door that opened onto the covered porch that circled the front of the house. Helen never knew how many boys would slip into their bedroom at night, nor did she care. Each morning before breakfast she peeked into the boys' room for a head count and then prepared enough breakfast for everyone.

It was Jerry's love for people that would drive him and motivate his entire Christian life. It was the reason why as a young pastor he knocked on one hundred doors a day, six days a week, and didn't care how many times those doors were slammed in his face. It is the reason he accepted every invitation to go on television and present Jesus, even if it meant being ridiculed. It's the reason he was willing to look like a fool for the sake of the gospel.

This love came to Jerry through his father. Two years before Jerry and Gene were born, Carey's younger brother met with tragedy. Garland, a happy and kind young man, had gotten caught up in a lifestyle of drugs and alcohol that kept him in and out of trouble with the law. Garland's older brothers had tried to protect him from himself. They bailed him out of jail and shielded him from the police as much as possible.

But on December 28, 1931, the police were once more after Garland. Paranoid from both the substances he abused and from trying to stay one step ahead of the law, Garland became convinced that Carey had reported him to the police. Nothing could have been further from the truth, but Garland had a gun and was in no mood to talk. He tried to shoot Carey, who escaped and ran for his life.

Garland, unwilling to stop his pursuit, went after him. The drama ended when Garland cornered Carey in the office of the restaurant belonging to their brother Warren. Somebody was going to die that day, and had Carey not grabbed a .38 Remington, wheeled around, and fired, it would have been him.

The police ruled the shooting self-defense and no charges were filed. Carey, however, judged himself guilty. He loved his younger brother and mourned his death for the rest of his life. After the shooting, he started his own downward spiral of drinking that would end in his premature death.

Carey's friends say that when he got drunk late at night he often talked about and wept over his brother's death. One night, as several of his friends sat drinking around the kitchen table, Carey, tears streaming down his face, said, "If you ever have to kill someone, just kill yourself instead."

In a way, that's what Carey Falwell did. Never able to overcome the guilt, Carey drank himself into an early grave.

The Power of Prayer

Carey's wife, Helen, was a wise woman. She tried on numerous occasions to tell her husband about how a black heart could be made white again, but Carey would stop her. "I don't know about that," he said. "I just don't know."

Because she understood the grief that drove his drinking, Helen never scolded her husband or said anything unkind to him. She held him, loved him, and helped him as best she could. And, most important, she prayed for him every day of his life.

With each passing year, Carey's drinking took a greater toll on his body, and although Gene and Jerry didn't understand it at the time, their father was dying of cirrhosis of the liver. Carey's cousin Virginia McKenna was the only person who wasn't afraid to talk to him about his drinking and his soul.

"Stop this, Carey, and go to church!" she begged. But he refused to listen. By the time Jerry and Gene were fifteen, Carey was on his deathbed. In September 1948, Virginia met one of Carey's old friends, Frank Buford, in the grocery store.

"Carey's awful sick, Frank," she said. "Why don't you go see him?"

"I'll do that, Virginia."

"And Frank, please say something to Carey about his soul."

True to his word, Frank went to visit. "Carey, do you remember telling me one time that if there was ever anything I needed all I had to do was ask?"

"As you can see, I'm laid up in this bed, Frank. But if there's anything I can do for you, I'll do it."

"There is, Carey. I want you to join the church."

"I'll do it," Carey announced. "Just bring the man."

Frank knew Carey was referring to Andrew Ponton, pastor of Jehovah Jireh Presbyterian Church. Frank left the Falwell house and drove to talk to the old minister, who agreed to go visit Carey the following morning. Pastor Ponton was so frail that Frank almost had to carry him into Carey's bedroom.

That morning, with Andrew Ponton and Frank Buford as witnesses, Carey Falwell confessed all his sins, repented before God, and invited Jesus to be the Lord of his life. In a stroke of divine love, his heart was washed clean by the blood of the lamb—Jesus— who was slain for the sins of the world.

For the next two weeks, until his death, Carey Falwell was a transformed man. Joy radiated from his eyes even as his body failed him. The guilt was gone and his demeanor changed. He was no longer demanding, but thankful to God and to his family.

On October 10, 1948, Carey died a peaceful man. As Jerry

sobbed in his pillow, he had no way of knowing the profound effect his father's life and death would have on him in the coming years. As soon as Jerry experienced his own transformation as a Christian, he understood that his father had suffered torment all those years for only one reason: no one was willing to brave his rejection and tell him the good news that would have set him free.

> *Not one Christian that I know about came forward to share the good news with Garland or my father in those early days. No one stopped my father or his younger brother on the street to tell them God's plan for their lives. No one knocked on the door of their homes or offices to share the plan of salvation or to place a Bible in their hands. Nobody stepped forward while there was time to save them. Then suddenly it was too late.*
>
> —JERRY FALWELL

The Intersection of Jesus, Jerry, and Me

"Is it as good as you remembered?" Jerry asked.

For a moment I thought he meant our life together, but he nodded at my soup.

"Oh my, yes," I assured him.

It was all good: O'Charley's, the soup, our life together . . . all of it. But surely Jerry knew that, as he'd known so many things over the years—not just about the past but about the future, as well.

Even before Jerry had a flicker of interest in spiritual things, it seemed the Lord had given him glimpses of His plan and purpose for his life. God had, as the Bible says, put eternity in his heart (Ecclesiastes 3:11). That was proved beyond a doubt one particular afternoon when Jerry was a teenager scrambling up the slopes of Candler's Mountain as fall colors shifted from green to red and gold. That unforgettable afternoon, Jerry sensed his destiny reaching out to him.

Jerry and Gene were together that day. The two were not identical twins. As they matured, Gene was the huskier of the two and Jerry remained rail thin. They differed in other ways, too. Gene loved to hunt. He taught himself how to kill and skin an animal. Jerry enjoyed hiking through the mountains, but he couldn't bring himself to kill anything. Gene had an amazing aptitude for anything mechanical, a gift that Jerry missed altogether. Yet for all their differences they had a bond that only twins enjoy, a silent knowing that one is part of the other, a connection so deep it did not require words.

Jerry and Gene often spent long summer days climbing through the maple, birch, sweet gum, elm, and dogwood trees on Candler's Mountain. But on that particular day, looking out over Old Baldy, something came over Jerry. A kind of knowing settled over him like a warm blanket on a snowy night. Something about the mountain drew Jerry, compelling him to look at it much the way Moses must have once looked at a burning bush.

"Someday I'm going to own that mountain," Jerry said with awe. "I don't know what I'm going to do with it, but I'll own it."

Jerry didn't even know God, yet the Lord had stamped His plan for Jerry's life so deep inside him that it was drawing him to his destiny. Jerry's prediction came true. Years later he did buy it. Today it's called Liberty Mountain and is part of the 5,000 sprawling acres that house Liberty University.

A New Day

Following his graduation from high school, Jerry enrolled at Lynchburg College after receiving a math scholarship. He was smart and had a photographic memory. He excelled in math and physics and could do anything he wanted with his life. In spite of his escapades Jerry was very shy, like his mother. When planning his career, he looked at his options based on one thing: he didn't want any career that required public speaking. Not that such speaking would be necessary. He was considered the greatest mathematical mind to have attended Lynchburg College. His gift was numbers, not words.

Since his glimpses into the future had been incomplete, Jerry had no way of knowing that his plans did not fit with God's plan. He had no idea then that God even had a plan. Nor did he know that his mother, Helen, and his aunt, Virginia, had made him the focus of their prayers.

January 20, 1952, began like any other Sunday morning. Jerry woke to the smell of hotcakes, molasses, and bacon. He knew it was his mother's way of getting him downstairs to hear the *Old Fashioned Revival Hour*. The volume was turned so high that from his bed he heard the choir sing "Heavenly Sunshine." He didn't want to listen to Dr. Fuller preach, but the food drew him downstairs. For the first time, as Dr. Fuller preached, Jerry felt a lump form in his throat. He was excited, yet weepy and edgy. God's presence filled every molecule of the kitchen, where Helen had spent years crying out to God for her son.

Still resisting the Holy Spirit, Jerry refused to go to church with his mother. Instead, he drove to the Pickeral Café, where he sat alone. Later, he wandered across the street to join the Wall Gang. That evening, in the middle of their conversation, Jerry blurted the last question he ever imagined asking.

"Does anybody know a church in Lynchburg that preaches what Dr. Fuller preaches on the radio?"

"Yeah," Otis Wright said, "a church over on Park Avenue. It's kind of a Holy Roller–type church, but they have good music and pretty girls."

"So why don't we go?" Jerry asked.

Jim Moon and Otis Wright drove with Jerry to Park Avenue Baptist Church that night.

This was my church, you know. I was there as one of the pianists for the service. The sanctuary was almost full, and the boys were ushered to the front row.

Jim Moon pointed at me as I played my heart out on the piano. "I think I'll ask her for a date."

"Then I'll ask that one," Jerry said, pointing at Delores, who was playing the other piano.

God had other plans about that, too.

That night, Jerry and Jim knelt at the altar and gave their hearts to Jesus.

Neither of us knew that our lives were going to collide in a cosmic explosion that would hurl us into our destiny.

CHAPTER TWO

Beating the Odds

Helen Falwell opened her eyes as a floorboard in the old house creaked. A man's outline was silhouetted in the bedroom door. Sitting up on the side of the bed, Helen peered through the shadows.

"Son?" she asked, "are you all right?"

"I went down to the altar tonight at Park Avenue Baptist, Mama."

"Oh, Jerry . . ." A sob caught her throat. Pulling on a warm robe, she followed Jerry downstairs. With a fire sparkling and snapping to drive back the frigid temperatures, Helen and Jerry sat and talked far into the night.

Jerry looked the same when he walked into class at Lynchburg College the next morning, but inside there had been a radical change. He hungered and thirsted for God in a way he could never have imagined. Jerry wanted a Bible of his own, one he could study and underline. He drove to J. P. Bell's bookstore on Main Street and bought a Scofield Reference Bible and started reading both the Bible and Mr. Scofield's study notes. Jerry was ravenous for the Word of God. He memorized the Gospel of John and then the book of Romans. His quick mind and incomparable memory were insatiable.

The youth pastor at Park Avenue Baptist, Jack Dinsbeer, took him under his wing, and together they reached out to the Wall Gang, many of whom came to salvation as a result. Jim Moon had given his heart to the Lord the same night that Jerry did, and Otis Wright followed soon after. Jerry was baptized in a group of fourteen young people. Many of the Wall Gang would eventually go into full-time ministry.

Three months later, in March, God called Jerry into the ministry. He finished that semester at Lynchburg College and started making plans to attend the Baptist Bible College in Springfield, Missouri. Until then, Jerry had planned on finishing his education at Notre Dame, after which everyone had expected him to go into the family business. In addition, for years before he died, Carey had warned Jerry's oldest brother, Lewis, "Don't ever become a preacher, son. People start acting funny the minute one walks into a room."

Lewis was now the head of the Falwell family. Lewis balked at the idea of letting Jerry go to seminary. On this matter, Helen intervened. "Let him go, Lewis," she said in her soft voice. That settled the issue.

Jerry would be the first preacher in the Falwell family.

He would beat the odds and break every stereotype along the way.

Against All Odds

In spite of the fact that I was already engaged to Julius, Jerry did everything possible to get my attention. But I knew the odds were stacked against us, even if he didn't. There was, of course, my engagement. But the bigger problem was that he was a Falwell, from a family of bootleggers and alcoholics. Born again or not, Mother didn't want me to have anything to do with him.

I didn't know Jerry well enough back then to realize that he loved to beat the odds, and Mother's resistance didn't deter him at all. What he didn't understand about me was how close I was to my family or how much I hated to disappoint them. Mother's disapproval alone was enough to make me shy away from him.

Although Jerry didn't know it at the time, he had an ally. My father, Sam Pate, had his eye on Jerry, and he liked what he saw. On the subject of Jerry Falwell, my parents' vote was split.

In the fall of 1952, Jerry moved to Springfield to attend Baptist Bible College. His roommate in the dorm was . . . none other than my fiancé, Julius. Jerry might have been born again, but he wasn't sanctified enough not to do everything in his power to come between Julius and me.

"I'm going to mail some letters," Jerry told Julius. "Do you have anything you want me to mail for you?"

When Julius handed Jerry his letters to me, Jerry destroyed them and sent his own. He conveniently forgot to give Julius my messages, and did everything in his power to stop our communication.

Eventually, Julius and I did break up, but not because of the lack of letters. I just wasn't ready to get married. After graduation from high school, I took a job at the bank. They needed a secretary and I was excellent at shorthand. I loved my work there, and over the next twelve years I would hold many different positions at the bank.

Passing the Test

I often wondered how successful Jerry would have been at building a church had he not first had the grueling task of building a Sunday school class of eleven-year-old boys.

The pastor of the local church in Springfield had seen too many seminary students and not enough success. The old pastor was disillusioned. So when Jerry reported for duty to help him, the pastor let Jerry know that he expected him to fail. Then he told Jerry to take over the Sunday school class for eleven-year-old boys. At the time there was only one boy in the class.

How hard could that be?

Most things in Jerry's life had come easily for him, but nothing he did seemed to get through to his eleven-year-old charge. Week after discouraging week passed with no results. Feeling defeated, Jerry went to the old pastor to resign his position.

"I knew you couldn't do it," the old man said, disgust dripping off every word.

That made Jerry change his mind. "I'm not quitting!" How could he ever pastor a church if he couldn't even reach one eleven-year-old boy?

He got a key to an empty dorm room and, every afternoon from one until five, he prayed for that boy. He prayed for his family and for God to help him touch lives.

By the end of the school year there were fifty-six boys in Jerry's Sunday school class. Up to a hundred showed up for special events. Teaching that class of boys was where Jerry learned that success required both hard work and prayer.

Beating the Odds

Jerry commuted 1,100 miles home to visit his mother and me. Despite my mother's objections, Jerry passed my radar test. Although I didn't want to hurt Mother's feelings, I wanted to get to know Jerry. So I started dating him without telling her.

One Saturday Jerry and I visited our good friends Billy and Iona Lynes. The guys were watching a ball game on television, and Iona and I were bored. I slipped Jerry's car keys into my purse and we crept out of the house, knowing that Jerry and Billy were so enthralled in the game that they wouldn't miss us for quite a while. Although I still didn't have a driver's license, I'd long since learned how to drive. So, I slid behind the wheel of Jerry's car and started it with no problem. The two of us were talking and laughing a while later when I looked in the rearview mirror and saw flashing lights behind me. Terrified, I pulled over onto the shoulder and stopped.

"May I see your driver's license?" the officer asked.

"I . . . I don't have one," I said, my voice trembling.

"Okay, I need you to . . ."

I don't know what caused me to look in the rearview mirror, but as I glanced up, I saw Jerry and Billy get out of the police car. *He set me up!* I smiled up at the policeman, put the car in gear, and sped away. Jerry and Billy walked home and we all laughed about it later.

In addition to the ally Jerry had in my father, he had won over both of my sisters, Jean and Mary Ann, and my brother, Sonny. When I went out with Jerry, Jean and Mary Ann covered for me. We dated during his trips home in 1953 and 1954. In time, Jerry beat the odds and won Mother over, too. He was finally allowed to come to the house to see me.

Not even wanting to please my parents could quell the practical joker in Jerry. One night after returning from a trip to Florida, Jerry spent the evening at our house. When the evening drew to a close, he said good-night and left. Our unsuspecting family fell asleep, unaware that Jerry had slipped back through the unlocked door with a large misshapen bag . . . that moved.

The next morning, I stood in the bathroom brushing my teeth and preparing for the day. Turning to leave, I screamed so loud that the neighbors heard me. An alligator filled the bathtub. Its beady eyes stared at me as its teeth gleamed in the morning sun.

My father raced to the sound of my screams, followed by my mother and siblings. Daddy looked at the alligator and breathed one word.

"*Jerry.*"

Lost in New York City

While Jerry moved out of the world and into God's Word, I spread my wings and for the first time experienced life outside Lynchburg. During summer vacations, my sister Mary Ann,

Peggy Mays, Mary Ann Williams, and I took road trips. I was the only one of the group who knew how to drive, and on our first trip I took us to New York City. I'd never ice-skated, but I tied on a pair of skates and glided around Rockefeller Center, laughing into the wind.

On a trip to New York City with my friend Charlotte Clark, I talked her into taking a walk. "We'll never find our way back," she fretted.

"I know the way back," I assured her.

We rambled through the crowded streets and sauntered into store after store. We listened to the taxi drivers blast their horns and smelled the rich aroma of food cooked by sidewalk vendors, our senses almost overloaded by the sights and sounds of the city. After a while, I looked around and saw nothing familiar. We were lost and I had no idea how to get back to the hotel.

I've always had a kind of radar that lets me know who can be trusted. Some may call it discernment, but whatever the label, it never failed me. As we walked down the streets of New York City, I scanned the faces of the people as we passed. I homed in on one man and knew, *He's someone I can trust!*

Over Charlotte's objections, I stopped the man and said, "Excuse me, we're lost. Can you tell us the way back to our hotel?"

"You shouldn't be out here alone," he said. "Come with me. I'll walk you back." After a pleasant walk, with a smile and a nod of his head, he left us at the front door of our hotel.

Meanwhile, Jim Moon, one of the Wall Gang who was born again the same night Jerry had been, joined Jerry at Baptist Bible College for the spring semester. When he arrived, Jerry and Jim roomed together.

"I wasn't as good a student as Jerry was," Jim recalls, "but Jerry wanted me to excel. Each night before a test, I would study a little while and then fall asleep. I slept on the top bunk and Jerry slept on the bottom. When I fell asleep, Jerry kicked the bottom of my mattress. He kept me awake and drilled me until he was positive I'd make a good grade, which I did. He always looked out for me, which was his nature."

In 1954, while on a visit home from Springfield, Jerry proposed to me. He slipped a half-carat diamond on my finger. I was crazy about Jerry, but I still wasn't ready to get married. *I don't want to hurt his feelings,* I thought. *I can always break off the engagement later.*

Jerry had no idea that I wasn't as committed to the idea of marriage as he was, but *if* I were ready to marry—which I was not—I suspected that Jerry might be the man for me.

While Jerry was at Baptist Bible College in 1954, both the pastor and youth pastor left Park Avenue Baptist Church and the church floundered. Saddened by the situation, Jerry took a year off from his studies to help. He drove one of his friends from Baptist Bible College, Frank Woods, to Lynchburg to take over as interim pastor, and Jerry took over as youth pastor.

After a year, Jerry went back to Springfield to finish his studies.

Fishing for Souls

Although Jerry knew that he'd been called into the ministry, he still wasn't sure whether he could preach. He'd preached to professors and classmates, but he'd never preached a sermon to people in a church. Without warning, two weeks before graduation, Pastor Zimmerman from the Baptist Temple in Kansas City told Jerry to take his place in the pulpit the following Sunday morning.

Jerry was scared and not at all sure he could do it. During that week, he prayed as he'd never prayed in his life. He prayed over his text and over each point of his sermon. He cried out to God to use the experience to show him whether or not he could preach. "Show me clearly, Lord," he begged, "so clearly that I cannot misunderstand what You are saying to me."

Jerry fasted and prayed the last three days before the service. On Saturday night, he prayed from sunset to sunrise. That morning, he stood before a crowd of almost seven hundred people and, without a single fear, preached.

Nineteen people responded to the invitation. The last person in line was an elderly woman with trembling hands and tears in her eyes.

"Young man," she said, "I am a charter member of this church. I've been sitting in these pews since Dr. Zimmerman started it. I've heard him preach and I've heard all the great preachers he's brought here, but this morning through your sermon God showed me for the first time that I've never really been born again. Will you pray with me that I might be saved?"

Jerry believed that God had answered his prayer, and the matter was settled in his heart. Dr. Zimmerman offered Jerry a position on his staff, but Jerry didn't believe staying was God's will, so he left Kansas City with no place to go. He was certain that somewhere God had a need for him to fill.

In the spring of 1956, Virginia McKenna bought two airline tickets to Springfield and then told Helen that they were flying to

Jerry's graduation. Since Carey's death, Helen had withdrawn to the house and seldom went anywhere. But at Virginia's insistence, she boarded an old prop plane and flew to Springfield. For years Helen had prayed for Jerry to be born again, and having him graduate from seminary was one of the great highlights of her life.

After graduation, Jerry came home to Lynchburg for a while before moving to Macon, Georgia, and working with a church there. He was preaching in Richmond one Sunday when more trouble brewed at Park Avenue Baptist Church.

Forging the Man Within

Years later, people were stunned at the strength and courage Jerry showed under fire during the Moral Majority years. Most people would have cowered had the attacks that were leveled against Jerry been leveled against them. They came by television, radio, the printed page, debate, and protestors. What most people didn't understand is that those criticisms didn't bother Jerry. He'd already been through the crucible of criticism in the early days of Thomas Road Baptist Church and nothing was ever that terrible again. This trial by fire, like all of them, forged him into the man God needed to stand against public opinion.

I arrived at Park Avenue Baptist Church that morning unaware that there was a change in the order of service. I gathered my music and started toward the piano when the interim pastor stopped me. "We're not having music today," he said in a clipped voice.

I slipped back to my seat and waited. He walked to the pulpit and announced, "We're not having music today." A buzz whispered through the sanctuary and a few people looked at me. *They think I won't play!*

Horrified at the implication, I made a small wave that rippled across the congregation. Before I could talk myself out of it, I stood and announced, "I came prepared, but he wouldn't let me play."

I sank back in my seat trembling. Something was wrong and the congregation seemed restless and uneasy. The interim pastor announced that there would be a vote that morning. Those in favor of him staying as the permanent pastor were to write yes on a piece of paper. Those opposed were to write no. Then he said that everyone had to sign his or her name to the vote!

One of the men stood and tried to speak, but he was not allowed to say anything. Because we were forced into a vote and not allowed to discuss it, thirty-five of us voted against him—me and my family included. After tallying the votes, he announced that he was the new pastor.

Then he told everyone who'd voted no to leave!

Shocked to be run out of our church, we just sat there for a moment too stunned to move. Most of those who voted against him were members who'd founded the church. Finally, with every eye on us, we stood and made our way out of the church for the last time. Others who had voted for the interim pastor to stay were so upset at how he treated us that some of them also ended up leaving.

We stood outside speechless. We'd been kicked out of our church! My father talked to Gordon Henderson and Percy Hall about starting another church, and Jerry's name came up as pastor. Jerry was speaking at a church in Richmond, so we piled into our cars and drove there to talk to him.

Finding the Right Road

When we told him what had happened, Jerry stayed cool and calm. He reminded us that he had planned on going to a church in Macon. However, he agreed to pray for God's direction. Jerry didn't take sides in the matter; he just sought the Lord in prayer asking for His direction.

After a great deal of prayer Jerry said, "I believe the Lord wants me to stay here and help you build this church."

In order to keep the peace and in hopes of mending fences, Jerry went to his friend Reverend Woods, who was now the pastor of Park Avenue Baptist Church. Jerry told the pastor that, though it had been his decision to send the dissenters away, there was no reason both churches couldn't work together in mutual love and support. "Why not turn this defeat into a victory?" he suggested. "Let the new church be considered a sister church of Park Avenue Baptist. We can pray and work together and both churches will grow."

> *When we were growing up, you just knew that there was something special about him. He was a natural leader.*
>
> —JIM MOON,
> ASSOCIATE PASTOR, THOMAS
> ROAD BAPTIST CHURCH

Pastor Woods seemed inclined to agree, but excused himself to call the office of the Baptist Bible Fellowship International, the ruling authority for the Baptist denomination, for their official stand on the matter. When he returned, he was no longer willing to cooperate.

Jerry was soon told by the Baptist Fellowship that starting another church in Lynchburg was unacceptable. He was ordered to leave town immediately.

Abandoned and Alone

The Baptist Bible Fellowship International, composed of the leaders of four thousand Baptist churches, felt that we thirty-five who had left had done so in overt rebellion. By agreeing to lead us, Jerry became associated with a rebellious faction and became bad by association. The fellowship issued Jerry the following ultimatum:

> If you do not leave Lynchburg immediately, you will be cut off from the Baptist Bible Fellowship International. You will not be welcome to preach in our churches or attend our fellowship meetings. We will not accept students from your church nor will our students be allowed to assist you in your ministry.

Jerry felt abandoned, cut off, and alone. The Lord said, "Stay in Lynchburg." The Baptist Bible Fellowship said, "Get out or else . . ." As he wrestled with the dilemma, the Lord made one thing clear: *You belong to Me and to Me alone.*

He stayed in Lynchburg and was excommunicated from the Baptist Bible Fellowship.

Harold Knowles was eighteen years old when he and his family left Park Avenue Baptist Church and helped found Thomas Road Baptist Church. "I applied to Baptist Bible College and they denied my application," he remembers. "They said they would accept me only if I went back to Park Avenue for one year. In the letter, they called Jerry a snake in the grass.

"I enrolled at Tennessee Temple in Chattanooga instead. For fifteen years, like Jerry, I was blackballed from their fellowship. Over the years, Jerry and I drove to Springfield to help get some of our students settled there. Each time we went to a restaurant, Jerry saw his former professors and classmates. They all refused to speak to him, and every time it happened Jerry's eyes filled with tears. It was excruciating for him, but he refused to disobey what he believed God told him to do, regardless of the consequences."

When Jerry looked back over his life, he cited this experience as the most painful thing he'd ever endured. He was twenty-two years old and had been a Christian for only four years.

Years later, when attacks came from so many different sources, their words didn't affect him. He knew it wasn't personal—those people didn't know him. But what his friends, classmates, and professors did was personal because they knew him and—even more important—he loved them.

The Bible promises that God will take what the enemy meant for evil against us and turn it to our good. Though we didn't realize it at the time, that's what God did in this situation. The enemy designed this attack to either get Jerry out of God's will or leave him so hurt and bitter that he was no good to God. Because Jerry didn't let either of those things happen, God forged in him the kind of backbone required to change a nation.

Donald Duck Baptist

Once Jerry heard from God on the subject of starting a new church, he moved us into an empty building that once housed the Donald Duck Bottling Company. We scrubbed syrup off the floor, cleaned, and painted while people in Lynchburg laughed at us. They called us the Donald Duck Baptist Church. There were thirty-five of us there that first Sunday morning, but Jerry told us that the church would double in attendance the following week.

On Monday morning, Jerry got up before sunrise and drove to the church. Inside, he pictured the sanctuary filled with people. He saw people sitting in theater chairs and standing along every wall. He imagined he could hear them singing hymns and praying at the altar. He got that picture so embedded in his heart that it became more of a reality than just thirty-five people in an old bottling company. It was there, on his knees, that he fought the real battle for Thomas Road Baptist Church.

Having fought the good fight of faith, he set out like a general to put feet to his faith through work. He pinned a map of Lynchburg to the wall of his cubicle office and put a dot at the church's location on Thomas Road. Using a felt-tip pen, he drew a circle around the homes in a ten-block radius of the church. Another circle mapped a twenty-block radius and a third circled a thirty-block radius.

Ever methodical, Jerry set his goals. Every day of the week except Sunday, beginning at nine in the morning, he would start knocking on doors. He would knock on one hundred doors a day, six days a week, guaranteeing that at least six hundred people each week would have a personal invitation to attend services.

Jerry took a pad and pencil for his own notes. He wanted to know who lived in what house in the surrounding neighborhoods. He wrote down the names and ages of every person in every house, listing their church affiliation, jobs, or schools.

God Must Have Sent You

Many people were rude to him, but he didn't let that stop him. He introduced himself as the new pastor of Thomas Road Baptist Church and invited them to attend. He wrote down all the pertinent information that he gathered about each family. And he left each family with a card with his phone numbers at church and at home.

"If you need to talk to me and I'm not at home," he assured them, "my mother will take your message and see that I get it." Even back in those days, Jerry was careful never to go inside a house if a woman was home alone.

Some people set their dogs on him. Others slammed the door in his face. But two or three times a day someone would say, "God must have sent you. I've been praying that somebody would come."

He encountered everything: couples whose marriages were imploding, sick children, alcoholics who had lost their jobs, and widows who were alone and frightened. Some people had been abused and others had been abandoned. Their problems were staggering.

Jerry read the Bible to them, counseled them, and prayed for them. He listened as long as they wanted to talk about their problems and then he asked God to intervene. He cared for those people and wanted to help, whether or not they ever set foot inside Thomas Road.

Jerry chose two men from the church and taught them how to go door-to-door. True to his word, by the second Sunday the church attendance had doubled. That success didn't cause Jerry to take a break and relax. He continued knocking on a hundred doors a day, six days a week.

The Triple Whammy

That first week, Jerry borrowed two old copy machines and, along with the help of a volunteer named Mrs. Hughes, he wrote the first Thomas Road Baptist Church weekly newspaper. Mrs. Hughes formed the headlines with press-on letters and typed Jerry's handwritten articles. He wrote about his dreams for the little congregation and mailed a copy of the newsletter to every person who had been visited that week. On Saturday afternoon, a volunteer phoned each home that had been visited. Jerry called it his triple whammy: a personal visit, a newsletter, and a phone call.

Large dogs chased him down sidewalks and on occasion someone shoved a shotgun through a torn screen door and pressed it into his chest. Each time that happened, Jerry remembered his father and imagined the kind of pain that would cause a person to act that way. He left, but he prayed for them.

> *I believe in ignoring the walls that people build. Behind the facades that separate us, we are all alike. We all need to know that God loves us. We all need to know that in Christ God has forgiven our sins and our failures. We all need to know that through Christ we can begin again.*
>
> —JERRY FALWELL

Ignoring Walls

A pastor of a local church called Jerry into his office. "Sit down," he said. "Now, the reason I called you here was to show you this." He opened a map of Lynchburg.

> *I never saw him lose his temper when he was dissatisfied. He held grudges for about five minutes and then he'd forget it and never discuss it again.*
>
> —DAVID RANDLETT, MINISTER OF MUSIC, THOMAS ROAD BAPTIST CHURCH

"This part of the city is yours," he said, pointing to the immediate area around Thomas Road Baptist Church. "I would like for you to keep yourself and your volunteers a safe distance from my church."

"Are you visiting those people?" Jerry asked, pointing to the area near the man's church.

"No, but that isn't your concern."

Once again, Jerry thought about his father and the needless years wasted in torment. "It *is* my concern," Jerry replied. "Those people are lost. I don't care where they find Christ, but if no one else is telling them the good news, then I and my people will do it."

Jerry loosened his tie as the heat reached triple digits and he trudged from door-to-door. "We don't want anything that you're selling, mister," he heard before the door slammed in his face. Sweat trickled down his back in rivulets as he climbed the steps to the next house.

"Hello," Jerry said to the man who opened the door, "my name is Jerry Falwell, and I'm the pastor of Thomas Road Baptist Church. We would sure appreciate it if you came by and visited our services."

"Well, Pastor," the man said, rubbing his chin, "I would like to go to church but I don't have any shoes."

"What size do you wear?" Jerry asked. Moments later, Jerry untied his shoes and gave them to the man. He made the rest of his visits that day in socks.

One Sunday not long afterward that man showed up at Thomas Road Baptist Church wearing Jerry's shoes, and he's still an active member today.

On the Air

In home after home, Jerry heard radios playing in the background during daylight hours and televisions blaring at night. Then one afternoon in the fall of 1956, Jerry and I were listening to music on a new country-and-western station, WBRG, when he remembered how God had used a radio broadcast to convict him and get him inside the doors of a church.

"Why can't we do the same thing?" he asked, thinking about a weekly time slot following the *Old Fashioned Revival Hour.* He drove to the radio station to discuss it.

Mr. Epperson, the owner of the station, was a Christian. He had another idea. "Go on the radio every day, Reverend. I've been looking for someone to start our broadcast each morning with words to the wise."

Old Time Gospel Hour cost $7 a program. On a clear morning that little radio station took our thirty-minute broadcast into homes across Lynchburg, Amherst, and Campbell counties and up and down the foothills of the Blue Ridge Mountains. Jerry announced over the air where he would be visiting each day and soon people were waiting for him at the door. He could sit in a small studio at the radio station and reach more people than he was reaching knocking on six hundred doors a week.

An Instant Celebrity

Jerry started broadcasting in September 1956, preaching on the air and bragging on God. People loved to hear him on the radio and then listen to him in person at the church. In December of that same year, Jerry started thinking about going on television. He approached the ABC affiliate in Lynchburg and agreed to pay $90 for a thirty-minute slot.

We knew nothing about radio and less than nothing about television, and there were no other preachers on television back then. The following Sunday afternoon at 5:30 we were on the air live. I played the piano, a man from the Methodist church sang, and Jerry preached. By the time we got to church that night the place was packed. Television made Jerry an instant celebrity. Before long, all of Lynchburg was buzzing about Thomas Road Baptist Church. No one called us Donald Duck Baptist anymore.

That first year of Thomas Road Baptist Church was the busiest of Jerry's life. He worked fourteen to fifteen hours a day six days a week and preached two services on Sunday. Like his father before him, Jerry's day started at 5:00 in the morning and by 6:30 he was on the air at WBRG. He slipped into his office at the church shortly after 7:00, and by 9:00 he was knocking on doors. Although his schedule must have been difficult to keep, Jerry had one of the greatest traits of a pastor: he loved people. He didn't have to *act* like he was interested in them. It was no act.

Setting a New Goal

The church grew so fast that we bought the little Donald Duck building and, with no collateral, borrowed $5,000 for our first expansion. Just before our one-year anniversary, Jerry announced his goal to have five hundred people in Sunday school the next week.

We were stunned. We'd started the church only a year earlier with thirty-five people. Back then it was almost unheard of to have five hundred people in a church service. On Saturday night before our anniversary, doubting Thomas that I was, I said, "Jerry, don't you think you're exaggerating a little?"

"No, I think we'll have five hundred people here tomorrow and break every record."

"But what if we *don't*?" I asked, trying to get him to be reasonable.

"We'll have five hundred," he said.

I sighed, hoping for his sake that we did.

By 9:00 the following morning, the sanctuary was full and ushers were filling every available space with folding chairs. By 9:30, people stood outside listening through the doors and windows while I played the piano.

"We hoped to have five hundred people here this morning," Jerry announced, "but we guessed wrong."

My heart sank and I felt disappointment sweep across the sanctuary.

"There are eight hundred sixty-four people here this morning!" Jerry shouted.

Pandemonium broke loose and I launched into the doxology while blinking back tears.

Pressing Forward to the Mark

That success did not slow Jerry down at all. Every afternoon, he took a break from knocking on doors and picked me up from work. If he'd already visited at least eighty homes, he would have dinner at my family's house before hitting the streets again. If he hadn't met his goal of eighty homes by the time I got off work, he drove me home, grabbed a hot dog, and started visiting again.

When the clock struck 10:00, he raced back to my house for a thirty-minute visit before my father knocked on the wall, his signal that Jerry had to leave. Jerry spent more and more of our time together talking about marriage, and I spent more time stalling.

By now Jerry had figured out that although my mother loved him, she couldn't stand the thought of one of her children leaving home. My sister Mary Ann had never married. But it was probably my sister Jean and her fiancé, Eugene, who made Jerry the most nervous.

They'd been engaged for years with no wedding in sight.

"I don't want to end up like Jean and Eugene," Jerry confided to one of his friends.

His concerns proved to be valid—Jean and Eugene's engagement lasted for thirty-six years, while Jean stayed home and nursed both my mother and father until their deaths. I suspect that, visionary that he was, Jerry watched their engagement stretch into decades and wondered if that might not be his fate. By now, I'd fallen in love with Jerry and wanted to marry him, but I still couldn't stand the thought of leaving my family.

My mother, with her subtle charm, did everything she could to slow the process. If Jerry and I talked about a spring wedding, she said, "Wouldn't a summer wedding be nice? You wouldn't have to worry about rain."

If we planned a summer wedding, she said, "Perhaps it would be wise to wait until fall when everyone is back from their vacations."

In the fall, she talked about how beautiful the spring flowers would be.

Another One Leaves the Nest

Mother was already shaken because one of her little birds had flown the nest. I had bought my first new car that year, a red-and-white 1957 Chevy, which I loved driving. I'd had the car only six months when my brother, Sonny, left for college. The whole family was heartbroken that Sonny would be gone for so long. When he packed to leave, Mary Ann gave him her checkbook. "Use it for whatever you need," she said.

Tears streaming down my face, I handed him the keys to my new car. "Take it," I said. "You'll need it." I knew as he pulled away in my car that Mother couldn't bear the thought of another of us leaving.

Finally, in 1957, Jerry told me that he'd waited long enough.

"Mother thinks we need more time," I said.

"Forget it," Jerry said, walking away.

I knew then that Jerry wasn't Eugene and he was running out of patience. I had to make a decision once and for all. It was time to choose between my old family or making a new one with Jerry. I had figured out that letting Jerry walk out of my life would be the worst thing I could ever do. The next Sunday morning I looked him in the eye and let him know I was ready to get married.

"When do you want to do it?" he asked.

"Next May," I said.

"March," he countered.

I pulled a date out of the air. "April twelfth."

"April twelfth it is," Jerry said with a happy smile.

When we told my parents that we'd set a date, Mother said, "Why not wait until summer when the weather—"

"April twelfth, Mom!" Jerry and I said in unison.

Drying her eyes on her apron, she accepted our decision.

The extension on our sanctuary was finished in March of 1958, leaving only weeks before the wedding for members of the congregation to paint, lay carpet, and install new windows and pews.

On April 12, 1958, dressed in a floor-length white gown and veil, I carried orchids as I walked down the aisle past a crowd of eight hundred with standing room only. The sanctuary was filled with fresh flowers, and Jerry stood in front wearing a black tuxedo. My father blinked back tears as he walked me down the aisle. In the front row, Mother sobbed. I'll admit it: I cried, too.

We had no idea the journey the Lord had planned for us. All we knew for sure was that we would take it together.

CHAPTER THREE

A Family Man

J erry, this won't do," I said, gazing at the wet towel lying on the bathroom floor and the socks and shoes scattered around the house. "Fold your towel and put it back on the rack." I picked up the towel to demonstrate. "And please put your socks in the hamper."

"Okay," he said with a smile. "I'll do it."

And he did. From that day on, a day very early in our marriage, he never failed to fold his towel or pick up his socks. For my part, I wasn't sure I could make the necessary domestic changes so fast or so well.

I didn't know how to cook. While my sisters had been learning their way around the kitchen, I'd spent countless hours practicing my drills on the piano.

How hard could it be?

One of the first things I did after returning from our honeymoon was to invite my sister Jean and her fiancé, Eugene, over for dinner. When they arrived, I had all the ingredients for a meal laid out on the kitchen counter. I had fresh potatoes and large steaks. Of course, they were raw.

I had no idea what to do with them.

While Jerry and Eugene visited, I pulled Jean into the kitchen and begged, "Show me what to do with these!" I watched while Jean passed the wand of her domestic brilliance over the food and presented us with mouthwatering steaks cooked to perfection, delicious baked potatoes, and everything to go along with them.

Jerry and Eugene groaned with pleasure as they pushed themselves away from the table. When the evening drew to a close, I hugged Jean good-bye with confidence that I could duplicate the meal. I had no idea that cooking was so easy.

To my great dismay, what Jean made look easy was anything but when I tried to do it. Jerry laughed as he cut black char off his steak and tried his best to eat an undercooked potato.

Surely there's something easier I can learn to cook.

Hot Biscuits

Jerry's mother made light, fluffy biscuits that melted in your mouth, and Jerry loved them. By then I had realized that cutting butter into a pile of flour and kneading it was beyond my current capabilities. But strolling up and down the grocery store aisles looking for *something* I could fix for Jerry, I almost broke out in the Hallelujah Chorus when I discovered biscuits in a can.

I can do this! I almost shouted as I scanned the directions. I even bought a pie plate to bake them in. At home, I pulled the pan of biscuits out of the oven and gasped with delight. Golden brown on top, they rose light and fluffy, almost spilling over the sides of the pan. I set the hot biscuits on the table and watched Jerry's face.

"Did you make these?" he asked, delighted.

"Yes, I did," I said, preening.

Jerry raved about the biscuits, but I noticed that he kept turning his head and pulling something out of his mouth.

"Jerry, what is it?" I demanded.

A sheepish look on his face, Jerry pulled a piece of plastic out of his mouth.

Apparently, you were supposed to take the plastic liner out of the pie plate before using it. It had melted into the biscuits. Jerry picked out the plastic and ate them anyway, praising me for my efforts.

Hamming It Up

Although, both of our mothers and my sisters would make culinary history for our holiday meals, I was determined to bake a ham for Thanksgiving. I called my good friend Dot Davis. "Tell me *everything* about baking a ham," I said. "Don't leave a single thing out." Pen in hand, I wrote down all of her instructions. Then, with meticulous care, I went step by step down my list. When the timer signaled that the ham was done, I pulled on mitts and opened the oven door. *It was black!* It looked like a huge lump of charcoal that Santa left for a very bad child.

I burst into tears, crying my heart out.

Jerry only laughed and would have eaten the thing had I let him.

I phoned Dot and she said, "You covered it with tinfoil, didn't you?"

"You didn't *tell me* to cover it!" I wailed.

Still not willing to give up, I decided to make a turkey for Christmas. *Finally, I did something right,* I thought as I set the beautiful brown bird on the dining table.

"Did you take out the giblets and neck?" Jean asked.

"What's that?" I asked, my heart sinking.

Jean reached into my beautiful Christmas turkey and pulled out the most hideous thing I'd ever seen. I was too nauseated to eat.

Country Gravy

I never cared much for southern cooking with gravy and sauces, but Jerry loved it, and I was determined to learn to make gravy. My next-door neighbor Kathy Combs made world-class brown gravy, so I turned to her for help. She gave me step-by-step instructions, which I wrote down and followed. My gravy turned out like bad oatmeal.

She went over the instructions with me again. Again, my gravy was a disaster.

Finally, I called her and begged, "Would you please stand beside me and tell me what I'm doing wrong?" She agreed, and stood at my elbow while I followed her instructions. "That's fascinating," she said. "You did everything exactly right, and the gravy is a disaster. I've never seen anything like it."

I threw up my hands in defeat. "That's it!" I said. "I give up."

Jerry took all my cooking catastrophes in stride, as he did everything in life. Jerry was a happy person, the kind of man who woke up each morning with a smile. He always saw the glass half full and never half empty. He never complained about my culinary failures and would have been happy to gnaw on charred meat.

Balancing the Books

Although I was not a happy homemaker in the kitchen, I did know how to handle finances. I'd worked at a bank for years and was appalled to discover that Jerry never balanced his checkbook.

"That won't do, Jerry," I said, looking at his checkbook register with dismay.

"Okay," he said with a shrug, "you handle the finances." Jerry's banker loved me because from that day forward he never had to issue us another overdraft notice. Jerry had a weakness about money: he wanted to give it all away. He couldn't say no to anyone in need, and he loaned money to so many people who never repaid that, in exasperation, I went to my boss at the bank and asked him not to approve any more of the loans and not to let Jerry cosign other people's notes.

Jerry left home one frigid winter morning wearing the black cashmere coat I'd bought him. He didn't have it on that evening when he returned home.

"Jerry, where's your coat?"

"Hmm? I don't know."

"You gave it away, didn't you?"

"Well, Macel, that man needed it more than I did."

Jerry was convinced that he could never outgive God. I was just as certain that he would *give* us into the poorhouse. Yet somehow we complemented each other's strengths and weaknesses.

On the Road Again

In years past, my three friends and I had gone on many vacations together. Not all of them as . . . interesting . . . as the one to New York, but all of them fun. We four had a trip planned to Montreal, but when the girls heard that Jerry and I were getting married they assumed our trips were over.

Jerry wouldn't hear of it, though. He not only insisted that we go, he gave us the keys to his new Buick. And so we went. Laughing and carefree, we never thought that we might need reservations when we arrived in Detroit late one night. We'd never had any trouble finding hotel rooms in the past, and we felt a bit like Mary and Joseph must have felt when every hotel we found had a No Vacancy sign blinking in the window.

"What are we going to do?" my sister Mary Ann wailed when the last hotel on our list was full. I had no idea. It was dark and late and we were in a strange city.

Just then a police car pulled up next to us. "Do you have a problem?" a young officer asked.

"Yes, sir," I said. "We've looked everywhere for a hotel room and we can't find one."

"Yes, ma'am," he said, "there's a big convention in town and everything's booked, but I have an apartment and I'll be working all night so you're welcome to stay there."

"No . . . *no, Macel!*" Mary Ann hissed.

I looked into the man's face and knew that he was safe to trust. "Yes, sir," I said. "We'd love to take you up on your kind offer." I followed him to his apartment, where Mary Ann and Peggy both refused to get out of the car.

"We're *not* going in!"

"Fine," I said as the other Mary Ann and I pulled our suitcases out of the trunk. "You can sleep in the car." Since I was the only one with a driver's license, I needed to get some good rest.

I thought they really were going to sleep in the Buick, but apparently they were more afraid of sleeping in the car in a strange city than sleeping in a strange man's apartment. When I followed the policeman toward the front door, they grabbed their bags and followed us inside, grousing all the way.

Inside, the policeman showed us around his tiny apartment before leaving for work. There were four of us, but only one bed. "We're not getting in that bed!" Mary Ann Pate and Peggy declared, crossing their arms and glaring at me. Mary Ann Williams and I shrugged, changed the sheets, and went to bed. The other two slept in chairs all night.

Early the next morning we heard a key in the latch. Someone was trying to get in. "See, I *told you!*" my sister whispered, looking for a weapon.

A man called through the door. "I've been working all night and I'm going to bed."

"You can't come in because we're not dressed," I explained.

"Who *are* you?" the man asked. "I live here!"

The policeman forgot to mention that he shared the apartment with his brother, a fireman, who also worked the night shift. I sent him away until we could dress and get ourselves presentable. By then the policeman was off-duty as well. The two men offered to take us out on their boat before we left for Montreal. Mary Ann Williams and I accepted their kind offer, and while we followed them to the dock, my sister kept up a constant litany of "I'm going to tell Daddy!" "I'm going to tell Mother!" But we all had a delightful spin around the lake before driving on to Quebec.

Setting Our Priorities

Back home, I went on with my job at the bank. Meanwhile, Jerry logged long days knocking on doors and preaching on radio and television as well as preparing sermons for Thomas Road Baptist Church. Still, we carved out many hours to spend together.

In those days, he asked me to critique his sermons. While I thought the content of what he said was wonderful, his delivery could use some work. Jerry spoke in a monotone and sounded somewhat nasal. At home alone, I helped him learn to put an inflection in his voice and we worked out the nasal tones. I helped him learn to speak in pictures. During each service I kept a small notebook where I jotted down any words he mispronounced. He appreciated the critique and never took offense.

Jerry and I talked for hours about our commitment to Christ. We studied the Bible together and prayed, asking God to be the center of our home. One of the things we spent most of our time discussing was how we were going to prioritize our life. How were we going to balance a family with a growing ministry?

"Jerry," I said, "I've seen far too many ministers take care of everyone else's children to the detriment of their own."

We made this a matter of intense prayer and the Lord helped us establish our priorities early in our marriage. We believed that our first priority was to God, and our second was to our children, though of course we had none yet. We determined then and there that the church and other ministry opportunities would not supersede our personal relationship with God, our relationship with each other, or our relationship with our children.

Making a Marriage

Early in our marriage, Jerry and I made an irrevocable decision that we would never divorce. In fact, we agreed that we would never consider divorce or even mention it as an option. Because marriage was a sacred covenant to us, we chose never to demean it.

That doesn't mean we didn't have our differences. We were very different people. But in almost fifty years of marriage we never once mentioned divorce. Jerry often said publicly, "Macel and I have never considered divorce. Murder maybe, but never divorce." He was joking about that, but he said other things that were no joke. One of them was, "Macel and I have had a million fights, and she's won them all."

Jerry honored me and deferred to me. He hated confrontation and didn't want strife in our home. He did everything in his power to make me happy. For instance, Jerry knew that I was afraid of

59

storms. During our entire marriage, each time he looked out the window and saw lightning, he said, "I'm sorry, but we'll have to finish this meeting later. I need to leave." Then he drove home to be with me.

On June 4, 1993, he phoned from the office and said, "Macel, go to the basement *now*!"

"Why, what's going on?"

"Just *go*!"

By the time Jerry got home, thirty trees had been uprooted on our property. The storm was so violent that gigantic trees were falling behind his vehicle as he drove into the yard. What woman wouldn't adore a man who would drive through a violent storm to get her?

Home for Christmas

In 1960, after renting for a couple of years, Jerry and I decided it was time for us to have a home of our own. We sat down with my brother, who sketched out a little ranch-style house with 2,000 square feet. We bought a lot for $1,800 and the total cost of our new home was $12,500. Daddy built my brother, Sonny, and his wife, Carole, a house just one door down from ours. I sighed with contentment to have family nearby.

"What would you like for Christmas, Jerry?" I asked as we made plans to celebrate the holiday in our new house.

"A baby boy," he said, longing in his eyes.

"What about a new coat or a pair of shoes?" I asked, laughing.

Jerry wasn't too good at keeping secrets, but I had become a master at it. The secret I kept in 1961 was a big one: I was pregnant. Jerry didn't know, and I went to great lengths to make him believe I *wasn't* pregnant.

Christmas Surprise

On Christmas Day, all of our family gathered at our new house to celebrate. After we enjoyed a huge holiday meal together, everyone started getting ready to leave, but I interrupted. "Wait, everyone. I still have one last gift to give Jerry."

I pulled Jerry in the bedroom, where he looked around for a gift. I put my arms around him and looked into his eyes.

"Merry Christmas, Jerry . . . we're going to have a baby."

Ever the practical joker, Jerry thought I was pulling a fast one on him. "What are you saying?" he asked.

"I'm three months pregnant."

"It isn't true."

I'd done such a fabulous job of keeping my secret that now I had to convince him of the truth. "It *is* true. I've been pregnant for three months, but I wanted to surprise you at Christmas."

As soon as he realized I wasn't kidding, Jerry pulled me into his arms and wept. "Can I tell the others now?" he asked, wiping his eyes.

"No, I think I want you to wait a while."

"Please?" he begged, and I knew he couldn't keep the secret ten seconds, much less ten days.

"Let's do it," I said.

Back in the living room, no one had moved. "Well, what did she give you?" Sonny asked. Jerry walked to my parents and said, "There's no 'maybe' about next year, Mom. We're going to have a baby!" My mother burst into tears and Daddy, knowing Jerry's propensity for practical jokes, said, "Are you fooling us, boy?"

"He isn't fooling," I announced. "I'm going to have a baby." Pandemonium broke out as family members laughed, cheered, and wept.

The rest of my pregnancy progressed just as the first three months had. I felt fine and went to work each day, doing the work I enjoyed. "I like my job and I don't want to give it up," I told Jerry as my due date drew near.

"Do whatever you want," Jerry said. "If you want to work, that's fine. If you want to stay home, that's fine, too."

Our Firstborn

On Father's Day, June 17, 1962, Jerry cried with every labor pain I suffered. Jerry Falwell Jr. made his debut at 9:13 p.m. In those days mothers were given so much medication that I had no memory of having given birth. Still groggy, I woke to a nurse handing me a baby and saying he was mine. I looked down and saw that my belly was not flat.

"That's not my child," I said.

"Yes, it is," the nurse insisted.

"No, I'm sorry, but you have the wrong room."

"This is your baby, Mrs. Falwell."

"It can't be," I explained. "See . . . my belly isn't flat."

Then, before she could turn away I saw the baby's fingers. They were long and slender, miniature versions of my own. I felt my heart clutch at the sight.

"Oh, yes," I said on a long breath of pure love, "that's my baby."

My sister Mary Ann had never married. In Jerry Jr.'s first weeks, every day when she left work Mary Ann bought him a toy. Soon Jerry Jr.'s toy collection rivaled a toy store's inventory.

Following my maternity leave, I went back to work and left the baby with Jerry's mother, Helen. But after only two weeks I realized that my child was changing in ways that I hadn't seen. Unable to bear it, after twelve years at the bank, I quit the job I loved to raise the boy I loved even more.

At home I rocked him and read him stories. When he got old enough I got on the floor and played with him. I made up stories like my mother used to tell. Our life was rich and full, and being parents to Jerry Jr. superseded anything we'd ever experienced. Jerry still shook his head in disbelief that I'd kept my pregnancy a secret from him for three months. "You pulled the wool over my eyes once," he said, "but it won't happen twice."

But, of course, it did.

Father's Day Surprise

I've always had an unusual gift of knowing about some things before they happened. One of those involved our children. I always knew we would have three children, a boy, a girl, and another boy. I knew without a doubt that Jerry Jr. would be a boy, and when I got pregnant a second time I knew I was carrying our daughter.

Once again, I kept my pregnancy a secret until Father's Day, this time in 1964. Jerry Jr., an active two-year-old, slowed down long enough for us to make Jerry a homemade Father's Day card. Jerry was drinking a cup of coffee when Jerry Jr. toddled over and handed him the card. Inside, the message read, "Dad, I'm going to have a baby sister. Her name will be Jean Ann Falwell and she's going to weigh seven pounds."

"What does this mean?" Jerry asked.

"I'm going to have a baby sister!" Jerry Jr. announced. The next thing I knew the two of them were chasing me around the kitchen.

I gave birth to Jean Ann, whom we called Jeannie, on my dad's sixty-fourth birthday, November 7, 1964, and the two of them had a special bond from the beginning. When Jeannie was just a little girl she said, "Mom and Dad, I don't love you as much as I love Papa, but when he's gone I'll love you that much."

Jerry continued with Jeannie what he'd started with Jerry Jr.— he prayed over her every night. And when she got older, he turned on her music box before leaving the room.

Another Son

Jerry was convinced that I could never surprise him again, but two years later I conceived once more and kept it a secret for three months. Jonathan was born September 7, 1966. I'll never forget the moment they put him in my arms with his shock of red hair.

"This isn't my baby," I explained. "There's been a mistake."

"Yes, Mrs. Falwell, this is your baby."

"No, we've never had anyone with red hair in our family."

He was, of course, our baby—a happy baby who smiled all the time. With three small children, our home was alive with activity day and night. I'd always felt that God had a two-pronged call on my life: to raise my children and to support my husband. I'd never felt so fulfilled.

Family Time

As soon as the children came along, Jerry cut back his late-night schedule and made a point to be home for dinner. Afterward, we read a story from the Bible and talked about its meaning. Following evening devotions, Jerry went to each child's bed, tucked the children in, and prayed for them. They adored those private times with their daddy, and it was then that they often shared their secret thoughts and feelings. As my mother had done, I read to the children and told stories to instill in them an early love of books. We held tea parties and built forts where they used their imaginations to explore the world.

Years later, when Jerry became president of the Moral Majority, he traveled 250,000 to 400,000 miles a year. But if I ever said, "I wish you wouldn't go," Jerry's response was always the same: he changed his plans. While his burning desire was to help save America's families, he wasn't willing to neglect his own to do so. His dilemma was that he didn't believe he could use his family as an excuse to sit back and do nothing.

In order to do one thing and not avoid the other, the ministry bought an airplane and he endeavored to be home for those evenings with the children. When he was on the road he talked to each of us at least once a day. Even when the children were grown and had families of their own he still called each of them every day when he traveled, and more often when he was at home.

Bumps, Bruises, and Broken Bones

Our children were all independent little people much like their father, so when four-year-old Jeannie, always daring, rode her tricycle off the porch, I was more upset than she seemed to be. "It's a greenstick fracture," the doctor explained after looking at an X-ray of Jeannie's arm. "I'm afraid I'm going to have to break it all the way before I can set it."

My stomach turned at the thought, and I wanted to weep for little Jeannie.

"I want you to look away," the doctor told Jeannie as he prepared to break her arm.

"Can't I watch?" she asked.

The doctor looked at me with shocked surprise. I sighed and nodded my head. Jeannie *would* want to watch. I cringed as the doctor snapped the bone in her arm.

"Oh, that's *neat!*" Jeannie exclaimed with wide eyes.

Soon after, Jeannie announced that she wanted to be a doctor when she grew up. At her tender age, she had no idea what a doctor did except break young children's arms, but she never wavered from her goal and is a surgeon in Richmond, Virginia, today.

Birthdays Were Sacred

Balancing family with a growing church was challenging, but one of the ways Jerry put his family first was to spend each of our birthdays with us. One time Jerry realized that his secretary had made a mistake and booked him to speak at a convention on Jonathan's birthday. By the time anyone noticed the error it was almost too late to cancel.

"We've made a big mistake, son," Jerry told Jonathan. "Here are your options. I will give you the thousand-dollar honorarium that I'll earn for speaking, or I'll cancel and spend your birthday with you just as we planned."

"I'd rather have our day together, Dad."

Jerry canceled the engagement without another word.

Sometimes, instead of just a family celebration, Jerry offered to take each child wherever he or she wanted to go on the big day. One year Jeannie asked to go to a particular restaurant in Danville, where Jerry surprised her with two little dresses that he personally picked out. On one of Jonathan's birthdays, Jerry took him to New York City where they saw Sandy Duncan in *Peter Pan,* toured Manhattan, and caught a Yankees game.

The White House

I was fifteen or sixteen when I overheard my parents discussing my birthday," Jeannie recalls. "Dad's secretary had made a mistake and he was scheduled to be at a meeting in the White House that day. I was shocked to realize that Dad was going to cancel his meeting with the president. 'Dad,' I said, 'I'm old enough now that we don't need to celebrate my birthday on the exact date. We can celebrate it the next day or on the weekend!'

"Dad looked at me and said, 'Jeannie, I've never missed one of your birthdays and I'm not going to start now.' He canceled his meeting and spent the day with me.

"In addition to never missing one of our birthdays, Mom and Dad attended all of our school plays, piano and violin recitals, and ball games. They never missed anything in our lives."

Daddy's Little Helper

As often as possible, Jerry took one of the children with him when he traveled. Back in the late sixties, a man named Gene Dixon gave the church a Cessna 310. This made it easier for Jerry Jr. to miss school and go to meetings with his father. By the time he was seven years old, he could often be found working the book table.

On a trip one Sunday, Jerry visited with a large number of people before remembering that he still had the key to the cash box. Hurrying to the book table, he heard Jerry Jr. shouting to the crowd, "You need my daddy's book!" Jerry Jr. had money stuffed in his pockets, down his

> *I was a kid riding in the car with Dad when we saw a man without shoes. Dad stopped the car and got out. "Where are your shoes?" I asked when he slid back into his seat. "Oh, I gave them to him," Dad said. "I have more at home." That was the way he lived his life: he helped people.*
>
> —JEANNIE FALWELL SAVAS

shirt, and in his socks. Alone, he'd sold $2,500 worth of books and records.

During that same trip to California, Jerry was injured playing basketball with a youth group and suffered a broken rib. Days passed in which Jerry couldn't take a breath without pain. He confessed that he was worried that the rib might break loose during the night and puncture his lung. Jerry Jr., convinced that his daddy might die if he didn't stand guard, stayed awake all night. Every thirty minutes he shook Jerry awake to check on him. That act of love sums up how all three children felt about their father: they adored him.

> *Mother had to be the disciplinarian because Dad didn't have it in him to be strict or serious. Once when Jonathan acted out, Dad tried to discipline him. Jonathan lifted his little fists to fight, and Dad just fell over laughing.*
> —JEANNIE FALWELL SAVAS

Summertime

In spite of the growing ministry demands, Jerry worked hard to give the children a normal home life. Part of that was providing family time during the summer. We bought a house on Smith Mountain Lake and tried to get away to it as often as possible during the summer months.

We'd often spend Friday and Saturday at the lake. Although Jerry Jr. was already in college, the younger children and I would arrive at the lake house as early as possible on Friday, and Jerry would drive down to join us as soon as he'd finished his Friday-night wedding rehearsals. He'd spend Friday night and part of Saturday with us before driving back to Lynchburg to officiate at a wedding or funeral. As soon as he was free, he'd drive back to the lake and stay with us until early Sunday morning, when he'd leave to preach the first service. We'd pack up and arrive in time for the second service. In spite of his schedule, he spent every available minute with the family.

Jerry loved family vacations where he had uninterrupted time with us. Perhaps this was because his time at home was often interrupted by hospital visits, weddings, and funerals. The first time Jerry and I traveled to the Holy Land we left the children at home with family. I stood in Israel with a sudden alarm ringing in my heart. "Something's wrong, Jerry," I said, struggling to stay calm. "One of the children has been hurt and we need to call right away."

Jerry and I rushed to a phone and learned that Jerry Jr. and Jonathan had been standing on a high wall when Jonathan had jumped. He was hurt, but would have no permanent damage. I don't know how many times I called to check on the children during that trip.

"The next time we go to the Holy Land I'm bringing the children," Jerry announced as we packed to go home.

"Why?" I asked. "That would be expensive."

A slow smile spread across Jerry's face and his eyes lit with mischief. "I think it would be cheaper than the phone bill."

We laughed about it then, but the more I thought about it the more I knew I never wanted to be separated from my children by continents. I decided that, especially while the children were young, if I traveled to another country I would take them with me.

Like Father, Like Son

When Jerry Jr. was twelve years old, he begged me to let him fly alone to Minneapolis, Minnesota, to surprise Jerry on his forty-first birthday. I did not want my son flying around the country alone but, with the logic that would later earn him a law degree, he wore me down.

"Don't tell Daddy I'm coming," he begged. He should never have feared; I had proved on three different occasions that I could keep a secret. With great reluctance I put Jerry Jr. on a little commuter flight to Roanoke, where he would take a connecting flight to Chicago and another to Minneapolis. Jerry Jr. made it to Chicago, but his flight to Minneapolis was canceled due to equipment problems. My twelve-year-old son was stuck in Chicago O'Hare, one of the busiest airports in the world.

> *A Christian leader's spiritual authority is established in direct proportion to the spiritual success of his or her immediate family.*
>
> —JERRY FALWELL

"Don't worry, Mom," Jerry Jr. said on the phone. "I'm going to check into a hotel and catch another flight in the morning."

I tried to get him to stay with someone from a local church, but he wouldn't hear of it. A methodical thinker, he worked the problem out in his mind and made it to Minneapolis, where he surprised his father. I don't know what delighted Jerry more, the gift of Jerry Jr.'s presence or witnessing his son's independence.

World Travels

On another trip to the Holy Land, I decided to stay home. By then I'd visited most of the places in the world that I longed to see, so Jerry and Jeannie left for an extended trip. Jerry Jr., Jonathan, and I stayed home.

After their tour of Israel, Jerry called me during a layover in Zurich and said they were going to take a day or two in Switzerland.

"Oh . . . I wished I'd come," I said. "I've always wanted to see Switzerland."

"It's not too late!" Jerry said, excited at the prospect. "Catch the next flight and join us!"

Fly alone? "Oh no, Jerry, I could never do that."

Jerry had such a love for his family that if any of us ever expressed a desire he was determined to fulfill it. Little did I know that after he hung up with me, he called Jerry Jr. "Here's what I want you to do, Son . . ."

Before I knew what was happening, Jerry Jr. had hustled Jonathan and me, our passports, and packed bags to the airport. I thought it was some kind of game until he walked out of the waiting area and onto the plane. Turning back, he urged me to come. I *couldn't* let my son go on a transatlantic flight alone, so I grabbed Jonathan and we followed him. Soon we found ourselves winging our way over the ocean.

Jerry beamed when we stepped off the plane in Zurich.

On another trip to Europe, our bags were checked at an airport in Rome when I said, "I've always wanted to drive across the Alps."

"Then let's do it!" Jerry said, excited to plan another leg to our vacation.

The only problem with our plan was that our luggage was already tagged and about to be loaded onto another plane. Jerry kept telling them that we wanted our luggage back, but no one understood English. Finally, we followed him to a warehouse area where we could see our luggage. I don't know what they thought we were going to do, but when Jerry grabbed it they almost had him arrested.

In addition to our family of five, we had Sonny's daughter, my niece Kathy, with us on the trip. Jerry talked to someone at a car rental agency and asked for two large vehicles. They assured us that would be no problem, but when we were ushered to the cars, we found that they were so small we each had to hold our luggage on our lap.

The cars were parked in the top of a large parking garage and we were almost dizzy circling our way downward looking for an exit, but we didn't find one. Because most people we'd encountered didn't speak English, Jerry didn't stop for directions. "We can figure this out!" he promised.

After an hour of circling the garage, Jerry's good humor had worn thin and he was frustrated beyond belief. Jonathan and I thought the whole situation hilarious and couldn't quit laughing. Finally, we learned that there was no exit from that building! We had to make our way to another part of the garage to find the exit. We all cheered when we drove out of the dark garage and into the stunning Swiss sunlight.

Driving through the Alps was like seeing a Technicolor movie in slow motion. One of the highlights for me was a wooden covered bridge with flowers spilling out over the sides. Jerry relished my delight. He loved the trip in part because I enjoyed it so much. We ended our journey in Paris and flew home on the Concorde.

Because my cooking was primitive at best, I was always thankful that Jerry was so gracious about eating anything I put on the table. During his travels, Jerry also strived to be gracious and eat whatever he was served. Although he preferred southern-style country cooking, as evidenced by his attempts to eat what I prepared, Jerry would eat anything. Jeannie went with him on a trip to Thailand, where—not wanting to offend their host—Jerry swallowed hard and ate his fish-eye soup. Then, as any good father would do, he noticed Jeannie's miserable face as she looked at the fish eyes swimming in the broth, and he forced himself to eat hers, as well.

Jeannie already adored her father, but that act of love cemented their relationship forever.

Road Trip

One of Jerry's greatest joys was making our dreams come true. If any of us mentioned someplace we'd like to visit, Jerry's response was always the same: "When would you like to leave?" In addition to traveling through the Holy Land and driving across the Swiss Alps, he took us to London, Greece, and Italy.

The year Jerry Jr. turned sixteen, he expressed an interest in the family's taking a road trip. It seemed as though he'd no sooner spoken than Jerry borrowed a friend's recreational vehicle and we were off to Niagara Falls and across the nation on winding two-lane roads.

At the end of each week, we found an airport where Jerry caught a flight home to preach the Sunday services. While he was gone, I drove the motor home to the location of our next rendezvous and picked him up from the airport. One afternoon I was in the back of the vehicle reading a magazine when Jerry sauntered up and said, "Hi, what are you reading?"

"Jerry!" I shouted. "Who's driving this thing?"

"Jerry Jr.," he announced, beaming with a father's doting pride.

Sure, Jerry Jr. had his driver's license, but handling a recreational vehicle was nothing like driving a car—it was more like driving a house. But once again, Jerry Jr. rose to his father's expectations instead of being held captive by my fears, for which I will always be grateful.

National Father Figure

One of the things we all loved about Jerry was that he never outgrew the kid inside who loved to laugh and play jokes. Still, when it came to keeping surprises a secret, Jerry was a big kid. If he knew what I'd bought one of the children for their birthday, for example, in his excitement Jerry would give them so many hints that they figured out their gift long before we gave it to them. That's why, when it came time to buy Jerry Jr. his first car, I had to keep it a secret from both father *and* son.

To the children, Jerry was just Dad. But being the oldest, Jerry Jr. traveled with Jerry quite a bit during the early Moral Majority years, and he grasped Jerry's role as a national and international figure long before Jeannie or Jonathan did.

"I didn't really know the extent of Dad's influence until I moved to Richmond to attend medical school," Jeannie remembers. "All I knew as a child was that Daddy took me to school every morning and was home for dinner most evenings. I had no idea that he flew around the nation and met with heads of state between breakfast and dinner."

Jonathan discovered somewhat earlier that Jerry wasn't like most fathers. "In the late seventies one of the hottest shows on television was *All in the Family*," Jonathan recalls. "I was watching it one evening when the main character, Archie Bunker, mentioned my dad by name! I was stunned. Then when I was thirteen I traveled with Dad to the Republican National Convention in Detroit. The two of us were sitting in a room when the door opened and President Reagan walked in, sat down, and talked to Dad. I thought it was cool, and I knew that didn't happen in most families."

A Heart for People

In spite of his national influence, at heart Jerry was a small-town pastor who loved people and never forgot a name or a story. Every Sunday he was the last person to leave the church because he stayed and visited with people as long as they wanted to talk.

"When I was twelve years old," Jeannie says, "I went with Daddy to Indiana, where he spoke in a large coliseum. As usual, Daddy stayed for a long time after the meeting talking to people, and I stood beside him. Years later, I happened to be standing near him after church at Thomas Road Baptist when a visitor walked up and said, 'I'll bet you don't remember me!'

" 'Oh, yes!' Dad answered without a moment's hesitation. 'I met you at the coliseum in Indiana. How is your son doing?'

"He remembered everything about that woman and her family. He had a phenomenal memory, and he used it to care about the people he met."

Nighttime Prayers

No matter where Jerry had flown during the day or how late he got home, he always headed straight for each child's bedroom to pray before climbing into his own bed. Jerry looked forward to his prayer vigil with eager anticipation.

He happened to be out of town the day Jerry Jr. decided to move into the dorm on campus. That night Jerry walked into our bedroom and said, "Where's Jerry Jr.?"

"He moved on campus today, Jerry."

"He did not!"

"Yes, he did."

One day Jerry and I stopped at a dry cleaner's and the woman working there said, "Jerry, you probably don't remember me. My daddy was . . ."

"I remember your daddy," Jerry said. The man had been dead for years, but Jerry reeled off his address and phone number. He never forgot anything about anyone he met.

—DUKE WESTOVER, EXECUTIVE ASSISTANT TO JERRY FALWELL

Jerry sat on the side of the bed and tried to blink back his tears. Jerry Jr. had moved only five minutes away onto the campus of Jerry's own university, but his empty bed marked a shift in our lives. Jerry had cried when I told him I was pregnant with Jerry Jr. He'd cried when I'd given birth to him. And now he cried because he could no longer tiptoe into his sleeping son's room, see his face, and pray a blessing over him each night.

Although he would never hold his children back, that night I believe Jerry understood what it cost my father to put my hand in Jerry's at the altar, and how hard it was for my mother to let me go. He had worked to make a happy home for our children, but already the first one had flown the nest. The others would leave, as well, and Jerry knew that one of the most delicious seasons of our lives was drawing to an end.

Death Is Part of Life

As happy and sheltered a life as we tried to provide for our children, we knew that trouble comes to everyone under the sun. Therefore Jerry and I tried to include the children in all the important matters of our lives, and death was no exception.

The children were only eleven, nine, and seven when my mother, Lucile, was diagnosed with intestinal cancer. She had been an integral part of their lives and they struggled to understand that she was dying. She was only sixty-three and we all still needed her. Jerry and I were honest with the children and managed to get them into her hospital room several times so that they could say good-bye. On November 9, 1973, she passed from glory to glory, and we all mourned her.

Left: Macel and Jerry share a moment during Thomas Road Baptist Church's second anniversary picnic in 1957. *Right:* Jerry and Macel were married April 12, 1958. Both were twenty-four years old and Jerry had been the pastor of Thomas Road Church for nearly two years. "We mutually committed to each other that night that this marriage was for keeps," Jerry later said.

The wedding party of the new couple. Jerry met Macel on the night of his conversion, January 20, 1952. She was playing the church piano and was actually engaged at the time. "I had my work cut out for me," Jerry later noted.

Jerry and Macel proudly show off their three children circa 1968. *Left to right:* Jeannie, Jerry Jr., and Jonathan.

A family photo of the family in the early 1970s. Today, Jeannie is a surgeon in Richmond, Virginia; Jonathan is the pastor of Thomas Road Baptist Church; and Jerry Jr. is the chancellor of Liberty University.

During a trip to Egypt in the late 1970s, the Falwells explored the pyramids on camelback.

Jerry Sr. and Jerry Jr. celebrate a great catch on a family fishing excursion.

Jerry and Jonathan about to embark on a sandcastle project.

Jerry and Jeannie, who he often called "my only perfect child," share some time at the beach.

Clockwise: A class photo from Jerry's high-school yearbook.

Soon after high school, Jerry began working at a local factory. This is his employee ID photo.

Jerry examines a line of Donald Duck Cola bottles. Early in its history, Thomas Road Baptist Church purchased an old Donald Duck bottling plant and converted it into a new church facility. Jerry said church workers labored many hours scrubbing the syrupy texture from the floors and walls.

Early in his evangelical career, Jerry embarked on a radio and television ministry. He is seen here in what is now the WSET studios in Lynchburg during an early broadcast.

Jerry Falwell having fun at a sack race.

Left: Jerry stands at the pulpit in the then-recently completed sanctuary that would later become the Pate Chapel, the site of many weddings and special services.

Below: Jerry joins with the TRBC audience in prayer during a service. He often stated: "Nothing of eternal importance is ever accomplished apart from prayer."

Jerry poses in the pulpit in front of a standing-room-only crowd at Thomas Road Baptist Church during a service in the early 1980s.

Jerry was always on the go and had the stamina of a bull. Here he phones the office while on a trip to speak in a church.

Jerry addresses the press at Heritage USA. The PTL scandal ushered in a dark period for the church.

Jerry was never afraid of having some fun. In addition to once going down the Heritage USA waterslide (in his suit!), he also tackled this bungee cord tower on a family vacation in Myrtle Beach, South Carolina.

Jerry meets with President Ronald Reagan, whom he called his political hero. Through the Moral Majority, Jerry steered the effort to elect Reagan to the presidency in 1980. *(Courtesy Ronald Reagan Library)*

Jerry sits next to President Reagan during a meeting of American religious leaders in the White House. *(Courtesy Ronald Reagan Library)*

Jerry welcomes Senator Ted Kennedy to Liberty University. Despite their many political differences, the two men grew to become friends.

Jerry appeared many times on Phil Donahue's talk show, which ran from 1970 to 1996. Their divergent social and political leanings often provided sparks that led to entertaining and informative broadcasts.

Jerry and Larry Flynt became unlikely friends years after Flynt's *Hustler* magazine printed a lewd ad parody.

Jerry meets with Israeli prime minister Menachem Begin
during one of his many trips to Israel.

Jerry meets with Israeli prime minister Benjamin Netanyahu during another Israel trip.

Jerry and Macel pose for a shot while attending a Christmas party with President and Mrs. George H. W. Bush. The couples became friends through the years. *(Courtesy George Bush Presidential Library)*

Jerry and Macel step off of Marine One after escorting President Bush to Liberty University in 1990. Marine One is the call sign of U.S. Marine Corps aircraft that carry the president of the United States.

Jerry and Macel enjoy a moment with actor and activist Charlton Heston and his wife, Lydia.

Appearing on the FOX News Channel's *Hannity & Colmes* broadcast. Cohost Sean Hannity has spoken at Liberty on several occasions and has become a close friend of the Falwell family.

Jerry appeared often on CNN's *Crossfire* series, here with Democrat strategist Paul Begala. He did this as part of his "salt and light" ministry, and he never failed to mention the need for America to turn back to Christ during his media appearances.

Jerry enjoys a casual moment with the Reverend Jesse Jackson and ABC News *Nightline* host Ted Koppel during one of his appearances on the broadcast.

Above: Jerry greets his dear friend Dr. Billy Graham at his North Carolina home. Three of Dr. Graham's grandchildren graduated from Liberty University.

Right: Dr. Falwell addresses a Republican National Committee event. He frequently worked to open political doors for the evangelical community.

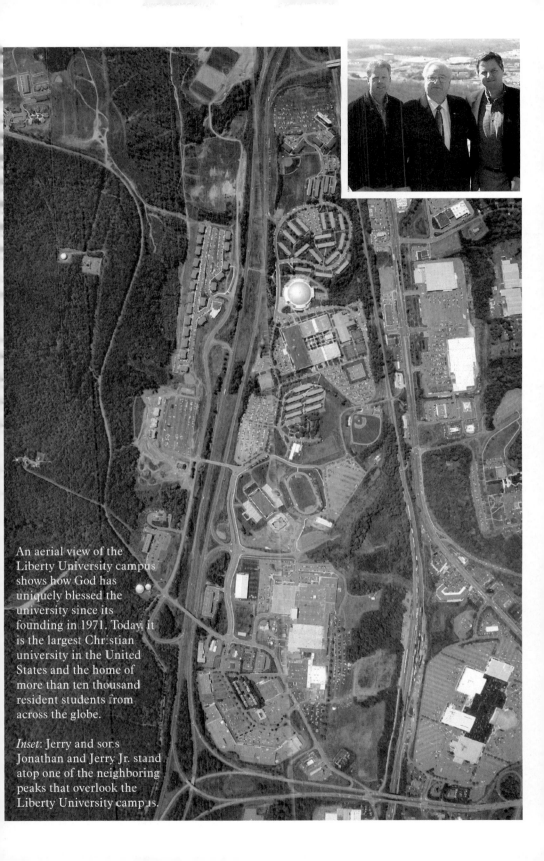

An aerial view of the Liberty University campus shows how God has uniquely blessed the university since its founding in 1971. Today, it is the largest Christian university in the United States and the home of more than ten thousand resident students from across the globe.

Inset: Jerry and sons Jonathan and Jerry Jr. stand atop one of the neighboring peaks that overlook the Liberty University campus.

Jerry greets Macel as she receives her diploma in 1987. She graduated with a 4.0 GPA.

Jerry and Macel Falwell

Jerry and Macel snuggle like teenagers during some private time. The public rarely got to see the softer side of the man.

Jerry and Macel enjoy time with their eight grandchildren while visiting the farm of Jerry Jr. and his wife, Becki. Jerry was known as "Poppy" to the grandkids.

The entire Falwell clan gathers for a family photo in the fall of 2006.

After lying in state in the Arthur S. DeMoss Learning Center's Grand Lobby, Dr. Falwell's remains were transported by horse-drawn carriage to Thomas Road Baptist Church, where his funeral was held.

The horse-drawn carriage traverses University Boulevard. Thousands of Thomas Road Baptist Church members, Liberty University staff, faculty, and students lined the street to pay their respects to their chancellor on this final journey across the campus.

In October 1976, Jerry's mother, Helen, was eighty-one. She was strong and in excellent health. But while entertaining guests one evening, Helen leaned against an unlocked door and fell backward, hitting her head on the table. Gene drove her to the hospital, where she appeared to have no more than a lump on her head and a bruise.

A few months later, in January 1977, Helen sat at home in her chair and listened to the radio as Jerry preached live from Thomas Road Baptist Church. Later, Gene found her still sitting there, unconscious. He rushed her to the hospital, but the doctor said she had suffered a cerebral hemorrhage. She lay in a coma for several weeks before dying on April 28, 1977, at the age of eighty-two.

That was the saddest day of Jerry's life.

Jeannie and Papa

Mother and Daddy had moved into our little house when we outgrew it, and they kept Jeannie's room just as it had been when she lived there. Following Helen's death, our children had only one grandparent left: my father, whom they called Papa. All three children loved him but there was a special bond between him and Jeannie.

The night of Jeannie's senior prom, she left with her date looking like a vision of loveliness. When she wasn't home by the appointed time, I began to fret. Finally, I woke Jerry. "Something terrible must have happened," I cried, frantic over my only daughter.

"Let's call the police and hospitals and see if there has been an accident," Jerry said. There were no accidents reported.

"Let's call the boy's parents," Jerry suggested. "Maybe they know something."

"He's asleep," the boy's mother said on the phone, after tiptoeing into her son's room and looking at his sleeping face. "He got home three hours ago."

"I knew it!" I wailed to Jerry when we got off the phone. "Something horrible has happened! How am I ever going to tell Papa that Jeannie is lost?" I paced, twisting my hands in despair. Finally, I took a deep breath and called my father. "Daddy, something terrible has happened. Jeannie's lost!"

"What do you mean lost?" he barked. "She's asleep in her own bed!"

"No she isn't . . . do you mean she's asleep in her bed at your house?"

"Of course that's what I mean! Where else would she be?"

I lowered the phone, limp with relief. How like Jeannie to migrate to her room at Papa's house on one of the most important nights of her life. His house was as much a home to her as ours.

Teddy Makes Two

Even with all the time Jeannie spent with Daddy, I felt he needed more companionship now that Mother had passed. Loading him into my car one day, I didn't tell Daddy where I was taking him, but I had a secret plan to get him a standard-size poodle. A friend of ours had the cutest black puppy, and Daddy and that dog bonded in a heartbeat. When the owner tried to take the puppy back he growled at her.

"That dog has never treated me that way before!" she said.

"He did it because he knows he belongs to me," Daddy explained.

"Well, you can have him, and there's no charge!"

From that day forward, Daddy and Teddy were inseparable. Once Dad suffered a slight stroke and fell, but Teddy wouldn't let rescue workers get near him. Guarding Daddy, Teddy bit anyone who got too close until my sister arrived and took him away.

Daddy recovered from the stroke, but Jeannie knew he needed exercise, so she took a walk with him every day. And each Wednesday she took him to Wendy's, which was Daddy's favorite place to eat because they gave Teddy a free burger. Daddy always kept a yellow Wendy's napkin in his pocket.

A Last Good-bye

When Daddy was eighty-four, he was admitted to the hospital with indigestion. He seemed to be stable so the next morning I talked Jeannie into going with me to help Jerry Jr., who'd just been accepted into law school, to move into his apartment. Jeannie was hesitant to leave Papa, but she went with me anyway.

While we were driving home, Daddy died of heart failure.

At his funeral, friends and family passed his open casket, paying their last respects to a great man. When everyone else had left, Jeannie stood for a long time beside his casket. As she said her last good-byes, she slipped a yellow Wendy's napkin in his hand.

Our lives were changing. We'd gone from a large, happy, extended family to losing our last living parent. Jerry Jr. moved away to go to the University of Virginia School of Law, and soon Jeannie was accepted into medical school in Richmond. Jonathan still lived at home while attending Liberty University and he traveled with Jerry as much as possible.

If we had any illusions that we would settle back and ease into old age, they were soon dispelled. We'd asked Jesus to live through us, and it appeared that He wasn't nearly through.

CHAPTER FOUR

A Church for All People

On July 3, 1973, the sun cast long shadows over Candler's Mountain. Trees drooped in the muggy heat. It began like any other day, but that would soon change.

As Jerry read the paper in his hands, all the color drained from his face. The Securities and Exchange Commission (SEC) had filed charges against Thomas Road Baptist Church for selling what they said were illegal bonds. The charges included fraud and deceit, and claimed that the church was insolvent.

The news rippled across the nation in headlines: S.E.C. Says Church Suffering from Gross Insolvency.

Jerry turned to Dr. Elmer Towns. "Elmer," he asked, his voice serious and solemn, "would you take the pulpit tonight? I can't do it."

The rumors alone were devastating. We'd worked for seventeen years to build the church, and charges such as these—even untrue—could topple it. The SEC had the power to force the church into bankruptcy, and to close our doors. We didn't want the case tried by the media, but in spite of our protests the journalists were having a field day.

For seventeen years Thomas Road had been touched by God's favor despite the odds stacked against her. Born from thirty-five people who'd been kicked out of their church and excommunicated from their fellowship, it had grown to an amazing membership of thirteen thousand. The television program, which had begun on one local station, was now broadcast over three hundred stations across the United States.

Those thirteen thousand needed Jerry. He counseled them, encouraged them, married them, and buried them. Together, Jerry and I made hospital visits and prayed for the sick. Jerry was still delivering the good news on radio and television. We'd started Elim Home, a ministry for men with alcohol and drug addictions, which had a waiting list of people seeking help. We offered a summer youth program for children in the community at Treasure Island, a Christian academy, and Lynchburg Baptist College.

Without divine intervention, one bond issue might bring it all toppling down.

A Time to Pray

The Bible says there is a time for everything under the sun: a time to be born and a time to die. Jerry knew that this was a time to pray. We would get legal counsel, but there was no question about it—only God could help us. Jerry had a pastor's heart and the idea of his sheep being scattered was too horrible to contemplate.

I remembered only one other time when he had been this exhausted, and that was in the early days of the church. Back then he was still pounding on a hundred doors a day, six days a week, as well as preaching on television and radio. His efforts had doubled the church attendance the first week and by the end of the first year we had more than eight hundred people in the Sunday-morning service.

During those days the church had succeeded beyond anyone's wildest dreams, but Jerry had become physically exhausted and spiritually drained. Something was missing. He needed help, and God sent it in the form of R. B Whittemore and his daughter, Ann, who came to Thomas Road Baptist Church because they loved to hear me play the piano.

While I introduced them to my spirited brand of music, R.B. introduced Jerry to the spiritual sustenance he needed. R.B. wasn't impressed with the number of people who attended our services. He wasn't impressed with the number of doors Jerry knocked on each week. Nor was he impressed by the number of homes that heard the gospel by radio or television.

"What's happening between you and the Lord?" R.B. asked.

"Well, we're spreading the gospel to more people than ever."

"That's not what I'm asking," R.B. said. "I'm not asking what you're doing *for* the Lord in ministry. I'm asking about your prayer life. What's your *relationship* with the Lord?"

Being with the Whittemores wasn't easy. They challenged and prodded in a way that made you uncomfortable. And yet Jerry recognized that they had been sent by God to teach him how to make his spiritual life more deep and rich. While Jerry had friends and mentors, there was a void in his life left from the professors and colleagues who'd abandoned him and still refused to speak to him. R.B. taught Jerry more about the person of the Holy Spirit than he had ever learned in school.

Jerry always dreamed big, and there weren't enough hours in the day for him to do all that he had in his heart to do. But, running on exhaustion, he needed a God-sized dose of supernatural strength and energy. What R.B. thought he needed was to tap into the secret place of the most High that the Bible talked about, where he could be in intimate contact with the third member of the Trinity.

He needed to find that place of spiritual rest where he could be recharged and refilled after giving all of himself to the work of the ministry. It was R.B. and Ann Whittemore who taught him how to gain access to that secret place. You might say that they taught him the access code, for the Bible says we are to enter His gates with thanksgiving and His courts with praise.

Jerry had always been a man of prayer, but R.B. taught him how to draw from the deeper well of the Holy Spirit, primarily through worship. Two or three days a week, Jerry drove out to the Whittemores' elegant home and studied with them, and on Saturdays I joined them.

Drawn to the Mountain

Jerry was willing to walk the soles off his shoes to spread the gospel, but R.B. taught him one of the most important lessons any preacher must learn: how to balance ministry with equal doses of working and waiting on God. Although it wasn't his nature to slow down, Jerry soon realized that he had to stay connected to God through intimate prayer or else he would burn out. What a tragedy it would have been to start out in the spirit but end up in the flesh.

In addition to Bible study, R.B. encouraged Jerry to read about the prayer journey of Rees Howells, a young Welsh convert whose prayers brought revival and changed the course of history. He read *Waiting on God* by Andrew Murray, along with books by Watchman Nee, Martin Luther, E. M. Bounds, George Mueller, and Praying Hyde, among others.

With a bustling young family, Jerry woke early so he could have quiet time with God before the family rose. In those early-morning hours, he combined Bible study with prayer, and for the rest of his life Jerry prayed a minimum of forty-five minutes to an hour each morning. But his prayer didn't stop there. Standing in a steaming shower with his eyes closed, Jerry put his hands on the slick tile and prayed, each tile representing a member of our growing family. He prayed in the office and driving in his car. He prayed walking around the church property.

> *Spending a long time in prayer does something for you. It builds your determination to see issues brought to completion.*
>
> —JERRY FALWELL

But when he was troubled, Jerry's heart drew him to the top of Liberty Mountain.

Every great man of God in the Bible had mountaintop experiences with the Lord, and Jerry was no different. The Bible says that Jesus used to pull away from the crowd and go to the mountain to pray. Jerry understood that pull, for it was there on top of

Liberty Mountain that he wrestled in prayer with the weightiest matters.

Jerry prayed over every decision in his life. He prayed over where to go and what to do. In addition, he spent a great deal of prayer time worshipping God. He kept a short prayer list, a long prayer list, and a list of crisis problems. An action-oriented person, Jerry had learned to be still and go deeper in prayer. He learned to keep a conversation going with God at all times. He learned to pray everywhere, at all times, and about all things.

> *The real secret to Jerry's faith was that he refused to focus on the problem. He focused on Jesus.*
>
> —DR. ELMER TOWNS,
> LIBERTY UNIVERSITY

Once he knew what God wanted him to do, Jerry got up off his knees and didn't look back. He refused to let circumstances—those giants in his promised land—deter him. Once he knew God's will, the matter was settled for him, and he wouldn't lie awake at night worrying about it. He trusted God.

A Fearless Stand

It was those lessons in prayer that would sustain Jerry through the dark days in 1973 when the SEC filed charges against the church for fraud and deceit. Those two words, if true or even thought to be true, had the power to bring even the greatest man of God crashing down in humiliation.

Our problems began when a man who had experience raising funds for Christian ministries through selling bonds went to work for the church. In those days, churches sold bonds to raise funds for various projects, usually building campaigns. We needed to raise money then to fund what would become Liberty University and also to continue funding the television ministry. This man wrote up a prospectus and offered eight percent interest on the bonds. We promised to pay back the bonds within ten years. Within weeks, money came pouring in from people who listened to the *Old Time Gospel Hour*.

The lawsuit was filed the last day of a pastor's conference at which one of Jerry's mentors, Dr. R. B. Lakin, was speaking. Dr. Lakin, a wise old man with silver hair, had been the first evangelist to broadcast the gospel on daily radio back in the 1930s and 1940s. Before leaving Lynchburg after the conference, he gave Jerry some sound advice.

"Take a fearless stand, Jerry," the wise old minister said. "Where you are right, don't back down. Where you are wrong, apologize and make it right." Having delivered this piece of wisdom, Dr. Lakin said his good-byes and left town.

Later, when Jerry was ensconced in a meeting with lawyers and accountants, the door opened and Dr. Lakin walked in. "I have returned," he announced. "I was praying over in West Virginia when God told me to come back and help you."

Dr. Lakin knew there was nothing he could do about our legal problems, but the Lord had alerted him that Jerry was spiritually and physically drained. He canceled all his meetings for one week and just ministered to Jerry.

While we were embroiled with the SEC lawsuit, my mother was diagnosed with intestinal cancer and told that her disease was terminal. Those were dark days, and we identified with the words penned in Second Corinthians 4:8–10: "We are hard pressed on every side, yet not crushed; we are perplexed, but not in despair; persecuted, but not forsaken; struck down, but not destroyed always carrying about in the body the dying of the Lord Jesus, that the life of Jesus also may be manifested in our body."

Jerry forged ahead in his battle with the SEC while my mother began her slow descent into death. We'd been alerted to a potential problem in December 1972, when someone told the SEC that we were selling bonds illegally. The regional director had contacted us for information regarding the bond issue. In answer to their questions, Jerry showed them documentation that we 1) had developed a prospectus, 2) had sold the bonds, and 3) had been paying interest and principal, as we'd agreed.

In spite of that, in July 1973 they filed charges against us, and the headlines made us look like thieves. Jerry made a statement to the press in which he said, "The church has yet to find one bond holder who feels he has been defrauded."

Jerry was determined to find what, if anything, we had done wrong. We realized we had made a mistake by not writing a separate prospectus on the sale of general bonds to finance our television ministry. But that was an honest mistake because we didn't know it was required. Another mistake we made was putting in print that Lynchburg Baptist College was accredited. We had applied for accreditation, and we knew it would soon be approved (in fact, the approval came soon after the lawsuit went to court), but we shouldn't have made that statement before it was technically accurate.

The church was far from insolvent, as the lawsuit claimed. But the matter caused Jerry to take a hard look at our finances. He realized that we were, in fact, living too close to the financial edge. In addition, we had grown so fast that we'd used volunteers to handle some things for which we should have hired professionals. Having said that, not a single person had been defrauded out of any money, and no one had lost a cent. We had done everything we thought we were supposed to do, and everything we had agreed to do.

A Lonely Road

On August 9, 1973, Jerry was asked to appear in court to answer the charges. It was a hot day without a breeze to bring relief to the dozens of men who filed into the courthouse in three-piece suits already limp in the withering heat. The courtroom was filled to capacity. As the charges were read, Jerry cringed each time the words *insolvent, fraud,* and *deceit* were used. The SEC presented its case, which was slim, since it hadn't found anyone who'd been defrauded as it had claimed.

Legal counsel for Thomas Road Baptist presented their prospectus, proof that both interest and principal had been paid, and pointed out the obvious: no one had been defrauded. Late in the day, after both sides had presented their case, the judge asked Jerry and the legal teams from both sides into his chambers. There, Jerry suggested a solution of his own.

"Your Honor," he said, "here is a list of outstanding businessmen from Lynchburg who are all members of Thomas Road Baptist Church. Will you appoint them as our finance committee and let them report to this court while they guide and counsel us?"

The following day, on August 10, 1973, the judge made his ruling. "As far as this court can determine there is no evidence of any intentional wrongdoing by Thomas Road Baptist Church. Nothing has been said from the witness stand that taints the good name of Thomas Road Baptist."

The headlines shouted the news for all to see: Thomas Road Baptist Church Cleared of Fraud and Deceit Charges.

People in the courtroom wept. Even strangers on the street choked back tears as they cheered Jerry on. Back in the early days of the church, when Jerry was making his treks to the home of R. B. Whittemore, one thing that made him uneasy had been the Whittemores' propensity to say, "Praise the Lord!" But when the ordeal of the SEC's investigation and lawsuit was finally finished, the cry of Jerry's heart was exactly that: "Praise the Lord!" He knew the victory had been won as much on his knees as by his legal counsel. He didn't actually shout, "Praise the Lord!" when it was over, but alone . . . he wept.

Another Storm

Prior to the SEC lawsuit, another storm had rumbled across the nation, threatening Thomas Road Baptist Church and the core of our belief system. That storm was the dark cloud of racial conflict. Already the nation had been torn by riots and racially driven assassinations. But for those of us in the South, life remained unchanged. We had black neighborhoods, schools, stores, churches, restaurants, buses, parks, jails, restrooms, and water fountains.

Segregation was a way of life, but that didn't mean the lives of white people and black people weren't intertwined, for they were. That was particularly true for Jerry, who was raised with a black caregiver, David Brown. A kind and gentle man, David was closer in many ways to Gene and Jerry than their own father was. David had rocked them, diapered them, bathed them, fed them, and played with them. He was a quiet and steady influence in their lives, and they loved him.

In addition to David Brown, Jerry grew up with many black friends. Yet after spending the summer climbing trees, fishing, and riding bicycles together, it was normal—all they knew, really—for each to attend a different school. Those traditions were so woven into the fabric of society in the South that most people didn't look at the damage this dehumanization was doing.

Long before it became an issue at Thomas Road, Jerry experienced the darkest side of prejudice and recoiled from its ugliness. One of the first times this happened was when Jerry was sixteen and had gone joyriding in a convertible with his black friend Lump Jones, who had worked for the Falwell family as a mechanic.

Jerry got off the school bus one day as Lump drove up in Jerry's little English Austin convertible. Lump had it purring like a kitten, and Jerry took it for a spin with Lump as a passenger. Jerry flew around the narrow winding roads at high speeds until a little boy on a bicycle crossed the road in front of him. Jerry swerved and the car flipped end over end. Both Jerry and Lump were thrown from the convertible, and Mr. Duval Candler found them seriously injured and losing a lot of blood.

While Mr. Candler drove both boys to the hospital, Mrs. Candler asked several black families living on her property to clean up all evidence of the wreck. By the time the police arrived, there wasn't a single shard of glass or piece of crumpled metal left in sight. Everyone covered for Jerry, including Jerry's eldest brother Lewis, who told police that he had been driving a Jeep on the back of their property when it flipped over.

Jerry and Lump had both been dragged through gravel and dirt when the car flipped over, and both sustained serious injuries. Jerry lay in the emergency room in a great deal of pain, realizing that he'd caused the accident and everyone was covering for him. He knew he was responsible for Lump's injuries, but the emergency room staff treated Jerry, and left Lump untreated because he was black. At one point, Jerry heard Lump ask for a mirror and the response sent chills down his wounded back.

"Shut up, n——! You're not going to Hollywood."

The moment froze in time for Jerry as the shocking difference in the way Lump was treated sank into his soul. He was horrified and hurt. It wasn't until Jerry's brother Lewis promised to pay Lump's hospital bill that the black man was given any medical care.

The trauma of that experience was a sore that festered deep in Jerry's soul.

Another thorn was added to the wound when David Brown, Jerry and Gene's nurse, didn't show up for work one day. A single man with no family of his own, David had never missed a day of work. He was as steadfast a presence in the boys' lives as their mother or father. The morning that David failed to show up for breakfast, Helen checked his room to make sure he wasn't sick, but he wasn't there. She searched for him on the property, but he was nowhere to be found. After school, Jerry and Gene drove around looking for him.

Two days later, Lewis found David unconscious in the lobby of the hospital emergency room. David had been carried into the hospital three nights before, badly beaten, placed on a hospital bed, and shoved into the hall, where he'd been left untreated. He'd been beaten and a portion of his head had been crushed with a blunt instrument. He hovered on the brink of death.

When Jerry, Gene, and Helen arrived at the hospital, they found Lewis demanding that the staff treat him. Without his demands it is doubtful that David would have received any treatment at all. Two weeks later, David regained consciousness, but he'd suffered such extensive damage that he was never the same. He was as gentle as ever, but his speech was slurred and his responses slow. In time he made the painful decision to move to Connecticut to live with family there. The Falwell family never felt the same without him. Jerry never forgot that it was the color of David's skin that almost cost him his life.

Missionaries to Africa

Jerry was a student at Baptist Bible College on May 17, 1954, when the Supreme Court ordered desegregation. At the time, even though Jerry was outraged at the way his black friends were treated, most of us in the South didn't realize that segregation itself was evil.

But something else happened while Jerry attended seminary that left him feeling uneasy and dissatisfied. He listened as missionaries to Africa preached inspiring sermons about the need for missionaries in that nation, and many students responded to the call. What bothered Jerry was that no one said anything about reaching the thousands of African-Americans in the United States.

All his life, Jerry had been taught to believe in the separation of church and state. He believed that ministers were called by God for one purpose: to win and disciple souls. So even though he knew the nation needed to stop the atrocities against his black brothers, he believed those battles were for politicians to fight. He felt that clergy had no right to divert their energies from the work of the gospel and involve themselves in such worldly wars.

Yet, deep inside, a conviction had begun to stir in Jerry. He was beginning to believe that God held the church responsible for not taking a stand against evil in the racial conflict. This conviction warred against his belief that both clergy and the church should separate themselves from all political issues. He felt he could not yield to one without transgressing the other. It was a dilemma that would find its way to the forefront of Jerry's own conscience, and to the doors of Thomas Road Baptist Church.

The racial issue that had been simmering for decades reached a full boil across the nation by 1964. The call went out for ministers to take a stand on the issue. Jerry responded to these demands in a sermon entitled "Ministers and Marches." In the sermon Jerry said, "Our only purpose on earth is to know Christ and make Him known." It was a sentiment held not only by most Christians of the day but also by most politicians. Neither group believed the church should be involved in the high issues of the state.

Jerry went on to say that he would find it impossible to stop preaching the gospel and do anything else—including fighting Communism or participating in civil rights reforms. He never believed for a second that Communism should not be fought or that civil rights reforms should not be made, but he believed those battles should be fought by politicians, not ministers of the gospel.

Treasure Island

Jerry's stand for the separation of church and state caused some to brand him a racist, a Ku Klux Klan sympathizer, and more. None of those claims could have been further from the truth. For instance, Jerry had bought an island on the James River to be used as a ministry through Thomas Road Baptist Church. Named Treasure Island, it was turned into a summer camp and was open to all the youth in the Lynchburg area.

> *If the church had done its job from the beginning of this nation's history, there would have been no need for the civil rights movement.*
>
> —JERRY FALWELL

One day, sometime after the camp had been open, Jerry got a call from one of the church's largest contributors asking him to come to their home. "We drove down to the camp on the island yesterday," the woman began, with her husband hovering at her side, "and we thought we saw some black campers down there. Did you know there were black children on our island?"

"Yes, ma'am," Jerry said.

"Did the law force you to let them in?"

"No, ma'am. It was my decision."

She was aghast. "Is this temporary?"

"No, ma'am. It's permanent."

The couple offered Jerry an ultimatum: get rid of those black children or they would withdraw all funding.

Jerry smiled and explained that Jesus died on the cross for everyone, including those with dark skin. He said that Treasure Island was open to all the youth in the community, and that included black children.

While Jerry didn't believe it was right to take a political stand on the issue, when racism raised its head on his turf, he wouldn't back down. He refused to knuckle under to the couple's demands. They not only withdrew their financial support but left the church, as well. Jerry didn't lose a night's sleep over it.

Protests in Our Church

As courts forced desegregation across the nation, one unfortunate outcome was that many churches started private Christian schools as a way to keep their children segregated. In 1967, Thomas Road Baptist Church started a Christian academy and we were accused of having the same motive, but that wasn't the case. We never had a policy limiting enrollees to white students. The first black student who applied was accepted and that policy has continued over the years.

Jerry didn't start the academy in response to desegregation. He started it because God and prayer had been kicked out of public schools. He wanted Christian parents of all denominations and races in Lynchburg to have an option of sending their children to a school where the day could open with prayer and teachers had the right to pray with their students.

In Jerry's sermon "Ministers and Marches," he reminded his listeners that according to the Bible we are citizens of heaven. Excerpts from his sermon were published across the nation and he was labeled a segregationist, a racist, and a teacher of injustice, dissension, and distrust. Jerry never hated anyone and he never taught any of those things, and yet he would be smeared with those labels for the rest of his life.

Four months later, in July 1964, Thomas Road was singled out as a racist church by protestors from the Congress on Racial Equality. The teenagers showed up on Sunday, July 19, for what they called a kneel-in. Just before the 11:00 service four male demonstrators came to the front steps of the church carrying a sign that read, Does God Discriminate?

During the praise and worship time, the teenagers talked to the press and created a disturbance out front. Jerry sent an usher out to invite them to worship with us. We were well into the service and the sanctuary was packed, so when they finally agreed to come inside they were shown to seats in the balcony. Instead of taking seats and allowing the service to continue, they created a disturbance by having a loud pray-in. One of the ushers asked if he could pray with them, but they refused. One of the teens told a member of the church that they weren't Christians and never wanted to be. Their "pray-in" was an excuse to create a disturbance.

Jerry continued his sermon, and when the demonstrators told police that they planned to create more trouble during the next week's service, warrants were issued for their arrest. At the hearing, Jerry dropped the charges and the young men were released to their parents' custody.

Most of us resented those teenagers for disturbing our worship, but later Jerry admitted that they had shown courage to stand up for what they believed. Those same young men tried to integrate a popular white teen hangout, Dude's Drive-in, by taking some black kids inside. In the fracas one of the young men was knocked to the ground by angry white teens. While the young demonstrator lay wounded, another angry man drove his car toward him while bystanders screamed. At the last minute he swerved and missed the sixteen-year-old protestor by mere inches.

Those boys had looked around the sanctuary of Thomas Road Baptist Church and seen a sea of white faces—but it wasn't personal hatred that separated white and black Christians in the South. It was decades of social traditions. No one in Virginia could remember ever worshipping in a church of mixed color.

That's why Jerry knew there would be trouble when he hired Paul Tan, a young man from Indonesia, as a full-time member of our music ministry. Several families left the church because of Paul's dark skin color, but Jerry refused to back down.

Sucker-Punched

Even though Jerry admired those young protestors for standing up for what they believed, it wasn't their strident voices that broke Jerry's heart over the issue of segregation.

Jerry would realize later that the Lord had been dealing with him about racism for years. He'd broken Jerry's heart over the way Lump Jones and David Brown had been treated. Jerry had tossed and turned in bed when black converts from Africa had spoken to the students at Baptist Bible College. When Jerry had preached in Jamaica, Haiti, Puerto Rico, and the Dominican Republic, he lived, prayed, worshipped, and worked alongside his nonwhite Christian brothers and sisters in those nations. It troubled him that there were no dark-skinned brothers and sisters to worship and pray with us at Thomas Road Baptist.

Jerry had also been convicted when he was preparing to speak through an interpreter to deaf children at an orphanage in the Dominican Republic. "Reverend Falwell," the British black pastor said, "in your talk with the children, please don't make any reference to black or white." Later, after he spoke, Jerry asked the pastor why he'd been asked not to mention black or white colors. The man's answer pierced Jerry's heart. "Almost every white American pastor stands up before our children and tells them how impressed they are with their school. Then they say, 'I am white and you are black, but I feel such kinship with you.'

> *God may have used the Congress and the courts, the strident marchers and their noisy demonstrations, to get my attention, but He used the quiet, loving voice of Lewis to open up my heart and to help bring lasting change to me and to my ministry.*
>
> —JERRY FALWELL

"These children are not aware of any color difference, and I must try to communicate those thoughts with my hands. In the Dominican Republic, we are a whole range of colors from light to dark. Here, we work on our similarities, but you Americans point out the differences."

Jerry felt like he'd been sucker-punched with conviction. He thought of how the whites and blacks were separated by color in the United States and felt as though these children were righteous by comparison. He didn't know it at the time, but God had softened his heart and the soft words of one gentle man would break it.

Every Saturday morning, Jerry drove to Main Street and sat in a chair at Lee Bacas's shoe-shine business. Every week at 10:00 in the morning, an elderly black man named Lewis shined his shoes. A fellow Christian, the lines on Lewis's face and his gray hair spoke to a life well lived and filled with wisdom.

Every week the dialogue was the same. "I heard your sermon on television last week, Reverend," Lewis would begin. "I sure do like the way you preach."

"Thank you, Lewis. How are you and the Lord getting on?"

"So good," Lewis responded. "The Lord is so good."

Each week the two men shared their hearts and basked together in God's love.

Then one morning, Lewis lowered his voice and whispered a question that he dared not speak aloud. "Say, Reverend," he asked, looking up from the rag he used to buff a shine onto Jerry's shoes, "when will I be able to join that church of yours over on Thomas Road?"

For the first time in his life, Jerry was speechless. Because of his preaching on television and radio, black families had been drawn to the church, but none of them had ever asked to join. And none had ever asked the gentle question that felt like a blow to Jerry's solar plexus.

"I don't want to cause you trouble, Reverend," Lewis continued as his brush licked a steady cadence on Jerry's best shoes. "But I sure do like the way you preach, and one day I'd like to join Thomas Road myself."

Lewis didn't ask for an answer, because he was wise enough to know that there wasn't one. But for the next few weeks and months, Jerry wrestled with the question There was no good reason Lewis couldn't join Thomas Road. Jerry knew it and Lewis knew it. From that time on, Jerry sat in uncomfortable silence, and Lewis let him wrestle it out alone.

Finally, Jerry realized that right was right and wrong was wrong, and he had to take a stand for what was right even if doing so would come with a price. He remembered the families who'd left because he'd hired Paul Tan. He remembered the couple who'd left because he'd allowed black children into Treasure Island. He thought of the children in that Dominican Republic orphanage, and the Christians he'd worked alongside in Jamaica, Haiti, and Puerto Rico. This day, he realized, had been coming for a long time, and he would not refuse membership to godly men and women like Lewis.

Under God—he could not.

Soon after Dr. Martin Luther King Jr.'s assassination in 1968, the first black family applied for membership at Thomas Road Baptist Church. The board voted unanimously to accept them. A few weeks later, a black man was converted in one of our services and asked to be baptized. Jerry counted it a great honor to baptize the man, and the church took a solid stand behind him.

The next Saturday Jerry slid into Lewis's shoe-shine chair alive with joy. "Lewis," he said, "we baptized a black brother last Sunday night and admitted him and his family to membership at Thomas Road."

Lewis's big brown eyes brimmed with tears. Blinking them back, he said, "I know. I know. I guess it's time for me to come visit, too."

Lewis, along with his wife and family, visited Thomas Road often after that, but never joined. Until he died, Lewis was a faithful member at his black church, but he had been a spokesman for the Lord. It was not the noisy, strident voices and demonstrations that pierced Jerry's heart. It was Lewis who, in his soft, gentle voice, had dared pose the question God wanted Jerry to answer. Because Lewis paved the way, no man or woman of color was ever denied membership at Thomas Road Baptist Church.

Having crossed that color barrier, Thomas Road membership exploded. Between 1968 and 1970 the church outgrew the 1,000-seat sanctuary that we'd built in 1964. Our architect found a set of historic old church plans designed, but never built, by Thomas Jefferson. Expanding those basic plans, we built a sanctuary that could seat 3,200 people.

And build it we did. June 28, 1970, was the first service in the new sanctuary.

About the Father's Business

The new sanctuary brimmed with people, and our Christian academy, which served kindergarten through high school, had more than six hundred students. It wasn't long before *Newsweek* magazine claimed that Thomas Road Baptist Church was the fastest-growing church in the nation.

How had it happened?

We'd gone from a handful of dissenters who'd been kicked out of their church to the fastest-growing church in America. But as long as there were people in Lynchburg who'd never heard the gospel, Jerry refused to sit back and be satisfied. Instead, he launched what he called saturation evangelism. His goal was that Thomas Road Baptist Church would preach the gospel to every available person at every available time by every available means.

The scriptural basis for this evangelistic thrust was Luke 14:23: "Go out into the highways and the hedges and compel them to come in, that my house may be filled." Using that scripture as a launching pad, Jerry trained volunteers to witness door-to-door throughout Lynchburg and the surrounding counties. We created gospel tracts, Bible study courses, leaflets, bulletins, and newspapers. Delivering the materials either through mail or face-to-face, we invited our neighbors to church. In addition, we ran ads in the newspaper, on radio, and on television.

By 1971, we were distributing thousands of pieces of literature a week. At least 10 percent of Lynchburg's population worshipped with us, and another 20 percent attended on a regular basis.

In 1968, Jerry had also started a bus ministry to bring children to Sunday school. Jerry and two men began knocking on doors, asking parents to either bring their children to Sunday school or send them on one of our buses. Once he got that route established, Jerry took two other men and started knocking on doors in a different neighborhood. We bought old buses at discounted rates and hired a man to direct the volunteers. Before long, we had forty-eight buses bringing as many as 2,500 children and adults to Sunday school.

We also used hundreds of volunteers to call our Sunday school members. We trained sixty-one captains to direct our telephone volunteers, and every Saturday the entire list of Sunday school members was called and reminded of the next day's schedule.

Whenever the callers discovered that someone had a problem, they were able to arrange for a pastor to help. Our Sunday school grew to over 10,000 in attendance.

Pastors and ministry leaders from all over the nation wanted to know how to grow a church. Jerry organized weeklong conferences called "Building a Super Aggressive Local Church." Over time, thousands of pastors and leaders were trained in those conferences.

Defying all odds, Thomas Road Baptist Church continued to grow and its ministries reached far beyond the Blue Ridge Mountains.

CHAPTER FIVE

The Moral Majority

On January 23, 1973, the Lynchburg *News & Advance* announced the death of former president Lyndon Johnson. But it was another front-page story that day that caused Jerry to push his morning coffee aside in dismay.

"Yesterday," the article read, "in the landmark *Roe v. Wade* decision, the Supreme Court ruled unconstitutional all state laws that prohibit voluntary abortions before the third month. Feminists hail the decision as an important breakthrough for their cause. Right-to-life opponents of the decision promise to fight for a constitutional amendment banning abortions."

Like the fall of an executioner's blade, the Supreme Court's gavel legalized the deaths of countless unborn children. Although Jerry hoped that any moral person, with or without a belief in God, would hail the decision as morally wrong, informed Christians and Jews understood that it would bring sweeping spiritual consequences, which those Supreme Court justices did not grasp.

How could they? Unless a person believed in the God of Abraham, Isaac, and Jacob; believed that the Bible was the inspired Word of God; and had actually studied the Book, they could not understand that their decision had just opened a door for evil to sweep through our nation. Not immediately, for God's mercy would hold back the stem of evil for a while, giving America time to respond and repent. But, reading the newspaper that morning with an understanding of spiritual principles, Jerry knew that this ruling meant that our descendants would not live in the same free America that we then enjoyed.

Roe v. Wade threw Jerry into a dilemma of epic proportions, far greater even than the struggle against segregation. He'd been taught that the role of all clergy was to spread the gospel and stay out of the political arena. However, this legal decision was unprecedented. It raised a question for which he had no answer: If this is the way things are headed, what will happen to this nation if no one who understands spiritual principles involves himself in government?

We, the People

In the days and months following the Supreme Court decision, an outcry arose across the nation. New York's Cardinal Cook asked, "How many millions of children prior to their birth will never live to see the light of day because of the shocking action of the majority of the United States Supreme Court today?"

Cardinal John Krol, president of the National Conference of Catholic Bishops, said, "It is hard to think of any decision in the two hundred years of our history which has had more disastrous implications for our stability as a socialized nation."

Thousands of people across the nation—senators, congressmen, judges, mechanics, and housewives—recoiled at the decision. It all made Jerry think of Abraham Lincoln's words in the Gettysburg Address: "that government of the people, by the people, for the people, shall not perish from the earth." If the majority of Americans opposed this ruling, and yet it had been made anyway, what had happened to the government of the people?

Catholics took a courageous stand against the ruling. Protestants in general, and fundamentalists in particular, stood by in silence. The situation weighed on Jerry's heart and mind as he wrestled with how to respond. As much as he abhorred the ruling, with equal fervor he abhorred the acts of violence that had erupted in response. The justices' lives were threatened and letter bombs intercepted and disarmed as people responded in blind rage, comparing them to "the butchers of Dachau" during Hitler's reign.

Crossroads of Conviction

The subject of abortion wasn't a new one. Many women—and even men—who had believed abortion was a quick fix for a messy problem had made their way to Jerry for counseling in hopes of finding a way to deal with the terrible emotional pain left in its aftermath. Jerry had read articles on the subject and talked to social workers, theologians, and medical personnel about the physical and emotional effects. Taking the only tack that kept him in his comfort zone, Jerry preached against abortion, calling it America's national sin.

And yet now he was at a crossroads. Jerry's own belief system demanded that he stay out of the fracas except to preach, yet he felt a growing conviction that God was prodding him to become involved.

He debated with God about it. He didn't have time for another commitment, after all. He was already leading a church of fifteen thousand members, blanketing the country on television and radio, writing books, teaching classes, and administrating the academy. He was speaking at national seminars, conventions, and workshops. Not only did he have no time or energy for politics, he had no *experience* in that arena.

Nor did most Christians, as evidenced when more than a thousand Baptist and other religious groups sent telegrams and letters to Associate Justice Hugo Black, condemning his participation in legalizing abortion.

Justice Black had died sixteen months before the ruling.

With growing uneasiness, Jerry realized that the only way to change the situation was to change the laws and change the people in office who made them. It meant getting involved in government, which meant getting involved in politics.

Finding His Footing

A scant eight years earlier, in his sermon "Ministers and Marches," Jerry had taken a public stand against clergy taking political action. In that sermon he said, "Government can be trusted to correct its own ills." The Supreme Court ruling made a mockery of those words, and he now realized that he'd been wrong. Yet he refused to step into the fray until he'd taken a fresh look at the Bible to see if he could find anything there that would substantiate such a move.

Jerry's fundamental dilemma was that the Bible teaches that Christians live in two different worlds. The first world is God's kingdom, which is invisible to the naked eye and seems like foolishness to those who do not perceive it. The second world is the physical one with solid ground, trees, oceans, flowers, and people, all of which can be seen and touched. As Christians, Jerry had been taught, we were to segregate ourselves from the affairs of this world. Now he was wondering if this was a valid, biblical truth. To find out, he went to the Bible.

One of the scriptures that he turned to, which ultimately changed the course of his life, was an account found in Matthew, chapter 22. The Pharisees, a leading religious group, had hatched a plot to trap Jesus in a public debate. The question they put to him was cagey. "Is it lawful to pay taxes to Caesar or not?"

They understood that, no matter whether Jesus answered yes or no, it spelled trouble for Him. If Jesus said, "Don't pay taxes," He would be arrested by Roman soldiers for defying the law. If He answered, "Pay taxes," He would offend most of Israel, who wanted the Roman government overthrown

As His answer, Jesus asked for one of the Pharisees to hold up a coin. "Whose image is on the coin?" He asked.

"Caesar's," they answered.

"Render unto Caesar what belongs to Caesar, and to God what

belongs to God," He responded. It was a brilliant answer that kept everybody happy

But, as Jerry meditated on this passage, he realized that Jesus had done more than just evade a trap. His answer was a commentary on the fact that, although our first allegiance is to God, we must still render to Caesar (the civil government) what belongs to him, meaning that we must still be responsible citizens willing to assume our position in *both* worlds.

Rendering to Caesar

Jerry stared at the passage, feeling convicted. All his adult life he'd done his level best to render unto God what belonged to God. But somehow along the way, he realized, he'd failed to render anything to Caesar, except to vote.

Jerry now saw that when we feel the laws of man's world are unjust or contrary to God's law, we must work to change them. In other words, he now believed that the Bible did support Christians' being involved in government.

But he still didn't rush out and jump on the bandwagon. He knew that becoming involved meant learning the issues and enduring the long, tedious political process. In addition, he led a church of fifteen thousand people, people who came from every political background and belief. He feared that taking a public stand on the issue would polarize his congregation. As a pastor, nothing could be worse.

Once again, it would not be the strident, angry voices that prompted Jerry to change his position. This time, it was the voice of a child.

Jerry and I talked long and hard about involving our children in the debate. At ages eleven, nine, and seven, they seemed too young to know that abortion even existed. Yet, if Jerry took a stand, it would affect the whole family, and we were both unwilling to leave them out of the discussion. During devotions one evening, with the family sitting around the fireplace, Jerry explained in simple terms what abortion meant. Jeannie asked questions and we answered them.

Jonathan, then seven, grew restless during our talk. After a while, he walked over to his dad and knelt before him. Lips quivering and eyes brimming with tears, he asked the question that would change our lives.

"Daddy, why don't you do something about it?"

Taking the First Step

*D*addy, why don't you do something about it?

Although the media always painted Jerry as an extremist, that was never true. Jerry was moderate in all things, including his political views. When Jonathan challenged him to do something, Jerry knew he must. But he didn't rush out and join the activists threatening the judges, nor did he stick his head in the sand and hope the problem corrected itself. His thought was, why harp about a problem when you could offer a solution?

Jerry believed that the solution was in the hands and hearts of God's people. He found the answer in Second Chronicles 7:14, "If My people who are called by My name will humble themselves, and pray and seek My face, and turn from their wicked ways, then I will hear from heaven, and will forgive their sin and heal their land."

In the summer of 1973, with that scripture as a promise, Jerry traveled across America with the Liberty Baptist College chorale, calling Christians to repent. A few years later, he launched musical teams from Liberty, who visited 150 cities across the nation presenting *America, You're Too Young to Die!* Through music, pictures, and drama, the concert called for change. These trips took place in several WWII vintage airplanes that were slow, but carried dozens of passengers.

"If the leaders of Christendom in this nation don't stand up against immorality," Jerry said, "we can't expect anyone else to lead. I believe it is the duty of gospel preachers to set the pace. When sin moves out in front, preachers and Christians everywhere must speak out. I will as long as I have breath."

In 1979, he kicked off a new musical tour, *I Love America!*, in Washington, D.C. That year, flying in old World War II planes, Jerry and the Liberty singers traveled to forty-four state capitols with their message. One photo from that era reveals Jerry at an *I Love America!* rally on the capitol steps in Little Rock, Arkansas, standing beside a young Bill Clinton.

Though hundreds of people across the nation sat up and took notice, more than a million and a half babies were still being aborted each year. The divorce rate soared, while pornography and drugs flooded the country. Jerry had to concede that it would take more than music and drama to mobilize the American people to help govern their nation.

The Moral Majority Is Born

There were political conservatives operating in Washington, D.C., at the time, but they had no grassroots support. There were three television networks, which made a handful of newscasters the national gatekeepers of what people heard on the news. The nation had no idea what was happening unless someone like Walter Cronkite decided to communicate it to them.

A Gallup poll in 1976 revealed that 60 to 70 million Americans considered themselves Christians. If even a fraction of that number were to mobilize, they could make a powerful impact. But how could they be mobilized so long as a liberal media controlled the airwaves? Believing that nothing was impossible with God, Jerry prayed for direction.

At that time in the nation's history, there was no such thing as value voters or the Religious Right. As a group, Christian conservatives had never been factored into national politics. These were good, solid Americans who went to church, took care of their families, and believed that voting was too worldly to do. There was no Religious Right because most of that huge section of America wasn't even registered to vote. Jerry's first goal became to get that sleeping segment of America voting—and not just voting a straight ticket, but voting the issues.

In 1979, Jerry called a group of conservative leaders together in Lynchburg to discuss the situation. Over lunch, Paul Weyrich said, "Jerry, there is in America a moral majority who agree about the basic issues, but they aren't organized. They don't have a platform, and the media ignore them. Somebody's got to get that moral majority together."

The group they defined as the moral majority went far beyond just evangelical and fundamental Christians. It included Protestants from every denominational line, Roman Catholics, Mormons, and Jews, as well as atheists and agnostics with no religious affiliation but who disagreed with the direction our country was taking.

In June 1979, with those potential voters targeted, the Moral Majority was formed. Along with Jerry, that first board of directors included D. James Kennedy, pastor of Coral Ridge Presbyterian Church in Fort Lauderdale, Florida; Charles Stanley, pastor of the First Baptist Church in Atlanta; Tim LaHaye, pastor of Scott Memorial Baptist Church in El Cajon, California; and Greg Dixon, pastor of the Indianapolis Baptist Temple. Their platform was pro-life, pro–traditional family, pro-morality, and pro-America, which included calling for a strong national defense and support for Israel.

The challenge before them was formidable: how do you mobilize groups of people who normally don't even speak?

Some people in our own circles warned Jerry, "If you do this you'll have to associate with Pentecostals and Catholics!"

"Yes," Jerry retorted, "and I'll associate with Mormons and Jews, as well."

He refused to let invisible barriers stop him. He worked hard to put together a meeting with leaders of every denomination and faith in order to ask them to mobilize their followers to vote. Standing before hundreds of religious leaders who'd never rubbed shoulders before, Jerry said, "I know that under normal circumstances most of us wouldn't even speak to one another. But these aren't normal circumstances. We've got to work together to save this nation. Afterward we can go back to arguing among ourselves."

Jerry borrowed $25,000 to organize a small office and get a mailing list going. He paid back the loan from donations and within a few years they had a multimillion-dollar budget and a rainbow coalition of their own that included people from every faith, creed, and color all working toward the same goal.

Calling People to the Political Process

What many people didn't understand was that the Moral Majority was never intended to be a religious movement. Groups of people who normally wouldn't speak to one another took their stand along Catholic nuns, who'c struggled alone for so long. Orthodox priests worked alongside Mormon elders and Nazarene pastors.

Jerry used television, radio, and the printed page to urge Christians to get involved in the political process. He told them to study the issues and vote according to their values. He encouraged Christians to run for office themselves, and he sent them out door-to-door to encourage Americans to vote. Jerry knew the federal laws, and he didn't break them. However, when Jesse Jackson began registering "nonpartisan" voters in the lobby of black churches (a legal but somewhat questionable practice), Jerry did the same.

> It is my conviction that what makes a good Christian also makes a good citizen.
> —JERRY FALWELL

Traveling thousands of miles each week, the board of directors purchased or leased private planes to help get Jerry home at night and back and forth to all of his speaking engagements. No matter how late, he always came home if he was anywhere east of the Mississippi River. Each time he landed in a city, Jerry called me with the phone number to his hotel room. I posted it on the refrigerator and the children were given permission to call him anytime they wanted to talk.

The Moral Majority held rallies and parades. They filled churches and convention centers. They produced television and radio programs. Jerry was interviewed by every major television and radio talk show host in America. The Moral Majority sent out massive mailings, manned telephone banks, and registered millions of new voters. They brought together 7 million conservatives who wanted to see a shift in government, and mobilized more than 100,000 priests, pastors, nuns, and elders to work together.

> Dr. Falwell could achieve objectives that his conservative mentors, allies, and friends only fantasized about. They were experienced and knowledgeable, but comparably impotent. He was fresh, new, innovative, and powerful.
>
> —DR. RON GODWIN,
> ADMINISTRATIVE DIRECTOR,
> THE MORAL MAJORITY

When former actor Ronald Reagan arrived on the national political scene, and his commitment to moral values seemed genuine, the Moral Majority threw their collective weight behind him in the presidential race.

Government by the People

The 1980 polls credited the Moral Majority not only with helping elect Ronald Reagan, but for voting eleven liberal senators out of office. One pollster said, "Reagan would have lost the election by one percentage point without the help of the Moral Majority."

In two years, the Moral Majority had created what had become one of the largest voter blocs in the nation—the Religious Right. Whatever label they were given, those voters were the "people" that Abraham Lincoln talked about—the majority that he wanted to have governing the nation.

In his address to the nation, President Reagan quoted 2 Chronicles 7:14, "If My people who are called by My name will humble themselves, and pray and seek My face, and turn from their wicked ways, then I will hear from heaven, and will forgive their sin and heal their land."

Ronald Reagan stepped into office at a crucial moment in history. No sooner had he taken his oath than the stock market dropped. Inflation rose and interest rates soared to 21 percent. In addition, the nation suffered from massive unemployment. Our

---

Of all the candidates our people supported in the election, not one was a fundamentalist. I would feel comfortable voting for a Jew or a Catholic or an atheist as long as he or she agrees with us on vital issues. And the private religious lives of elected officials are their business just as long as they keep their public responsibility to the voters who elected them.

—JERRY FALWELL

---

national defense system had been dismantled, we'd given away the Panama Canal, and American citizens were being held hostage inside the U.S. embassy in Iran.

A few months after Reagan's inauguration, Jerry and I sat in our car in the church parking lot listening to the radio. We'd been asked to stay tuned for late-breaking news that would interrupt regular programming.

"I wonder what's happened," Jerry mused.

I cannot tell you how I knew, but the answer was as clear to me as the names of my children. With wide, horrified eyes I turned to Jerry. "President Reagan has been shot."

"*What?* No, surely not!"

A few minutes later the radio announcer confirmed what the Lord had already revealed to me. The man "we, the people" had fought so hard to elect had just been shot.

Change Ripples Around the World

The nation as a whole was grateful that President Reagan recovered from the shooting. As a result of his two terms as president, Reagan was credited with winning the Cold War and bringing about the fall of the Soviet Union, one of the largest Communist powers on earth.

Unwilling to lose its momentum, the Moral Majority continued to get more conservatives registered to vote for the next elections and to educate Americans about the issues.

One of the men Jerry had hired on staff at Liberty was Dr. Ron Godwin. Ron had a Ph.D. in planning and management and worked as the administrative associate to the school's president, Pierre Guillermin. Ron had been working hard to help meet the needs of the growing college, and therefore he'd had little contact with Jerry as he'd traveled for the Moral Majority. Then one day Jerry asked Ron to drive up Liberty Mountain with him.

"Back then there really wasn't a road," Dr. Godwin recalls, "just two tracks up the side of the mountain that washed out when it rained. Dr. Falwell put his truck in four-wheel drive and it growled up that mountain. The view was spectacular. To the west we could see almost all the way to Roanoke. We had an expansive view of the Blue Ridge Mountains. But the view he loved was looking straight down on Liberty University and Thomas Road Baptist Church."

Dr. Godwin further recounts his talk with Jerry that day. By then Ron was calling him "Doc," after Jerry had been given the first of three honorary doctorates he would ultimately receive from universities and seminaries around the world.

"It was there," Dr. Godwin continues, "sitting in the spot where Doc loved to pray, that he told me he was going to lift me out of Liberty and make me the administrative director for the Moral Majority. At that moment my life shifted. I was a young man from the Deep South, not very traveled. I suddenly found myself driving to the Lynchburg Airport every morning, flying to Washington, D.C., and catching a bus to my office. Doc got so many invitations to speak that he divvied them up, and I found myself flying all over the world to represent him. Over the years, I spoke in fifty Jewish synagogues and met with thirty heads of state, congressmen, senators, and presidents, representing the Moral Majority.

"I worked with him every day for years and I still get defensive about the media labeling him as a right-wing extremist. I was privy to meetings among the very same conservative leaders who helped from the Moral Majority, and many of those guys were frustrated with Dr. Falwell because of his *lack* of extremism. He refused to get on their bandwagon. He always pulled back.

"After spending years in Washington," Godwin continues, "I learned how it worked. Washington is a sort of 'you scratch my back and I'll scratch yours' system. That's the way Congress works. It's the way the whole place works. I used to chide Doc because he would never call in his chips. He was always generous and helpful but he would never call in favors, except from God. He lacked political greed, and refused to play that game."

One morning Jerry had to catch a flight to Washington, D.C., to speak at a Right to Life rally. At the last minute he grabbed Ron to go with him. Thousands of people waited on the Mall, and a small area was roped off for the speakers. Jerry and Ron stood talking with senators and congressmen, when a homeless man leaned over the rope.

"Reverend," the man said, "I'm on my way to Key West, and I'm broke and hungry and I need food."

Jerry emptied his pockets and gave the man all his money. After speaking at the rally, he had a jet waiting at the airport to fly him home. What he didn't have was cab fare to get to the airport.

That scene was replayed in countless cities across America.

An Alternative to Abortion

One day in 1981, I stood beside Jerry as he spoke at a press conference. Afterward we left to catch our plane while security guards tried to control the crowd. A young female reporter shouted over the hubbub, "Mr. Falwell, one more question please!" Jerry turned toward her.

"You say you're against abortion?"

"Yes."

"But what alternative to abortion do girls have when facing an unwanted pregnancy?"

"They can have the baby," Jerry answered.

"Do you really think it's that simple?"

The crowd grew quiet and listened as the woman made her case.

"Many of the girls facing unwanted pregnancies are young and poor. Some are victims of incest, rape, or abuse. Some are just children themselves, and many would be kicked out of homes, jobs, or schools if the pregnancy is discovered. Some might even be beaten.

"What are you doing for women who want to keep their babies but don't know how to survive? They have no money for medical treatment, no place to live, and no one to support them. Reverend Falwell, is it really enough for you to take a stand against abortion when you aren't doing anything to help pregnant girls who see no other way out?"

The young woman's quiet question pierced Jerry's heart in much the same way that Lewis's question had that Saturday morning so many years before, when he'd asked, "Reverend, when do you think I might join your church?"

What are you doing for women who want to keep their babies but don't know how to survive?

Jerry didn't have to wrestle to find an answer to her question. The simple answer was that we were doing nothing.

Jerry came home from that trip and drew up plans for a new ministry through Thomas Road Baptist Church. He formed the Liberty Godparent Home. Any woman who found herself pregnant and didn't want to have an abortion could live for free at the home during her pregnancy. The girls were given the choice of keeping their babies or allowing them to be adopted through the Liberty Godparent Adoption Agency. Counseling was provided, and any girl who qualified academically was given a scholarship to Liberty.

> *Dr. Falwell was the exact opposite of what the media painted him to be. He was caring, nurturing, and incredibly warm. He was a visionary with clear-minded goals and objectives. He was generous, gracious, and decisive. Once he conceived something, prayed it through, and settled it in his heart, he didn't care what it might cost him. He didn't care about the obstacles. To him, it was already a reality and the rest was just mechanics.*
>
> —DR. RON GODWIN

Never one to dream small dreams, Jerry's goal was one day to have thousands of these homes across the nation. And so we set about trying to make it a reality. It took a great deal of work to get other homes started, and it required our working with different state and national agencies and departments of welfare, but every live birth made all the hard work worthwhile.

One of the first things Jerry did was to establish a pregnancy hotline to offer help to women with unwanted pregnancies. Late at night, one of the phone lines lit up and the volunteer operator heard the frightened voice of a young girl named JoAnn.

"My dad's drunk, and if he wakes up he'll kill me," she whispered.

The operator asked for her phone number and address. "I can't tell you where I am! If you show up here I'm dead!" With that she hung up.

Several hours later, she called again. "I'm fourteen," she said. "My mother was in a bad accident and she can't move. When I was eleven my dad started having sex with me, now I think I'm pregnant. My dad says he'll hurt me if I tell anyone, but I have three younger sisters and he's already having sex with two of them."

The operator convinced the girl to give them her name and address, but soon after that the line went dead. The next morning, social services in Detroit were notified of the girl's situation. When they entered the house, the child's father was still drunk on the sofa. The mother was paralyzed, and there were twenty cats defiling the home. The fourteen-year-old girl who had called was indeed pregnant, and two of her sisters had been molested. The mother's condition, the stench, and the evidence of physical abuse made it one of the more heartbreaking situations the social workers had seen.

JoAnn stayed at the Liberty Godparent Home for five months. JoAnn's story, and those of many other girls who called for help, cemented Jerry's decision that faith without works is dead. It wasn't enough just to preach—he had to act.

> *Where there is suffering we must act. And if our action requires political involvement, so be it.*
> —JERRY FALWELL

The Myth versus the Man

Some in the liberal media upped their accusations against Jerry. Once again the terms *hatemonger* and *extremist* blanketed the country. Political enemies called Jerry and Pat Robertson "agents of intolerance." Nothing could have been further from the truth.

Jerry's political beliefs were very middle-of-the-road. While he opposed abortion, Jerry would have accepted legislation that allowed it in the case of rape, incest, or if the mother's life was in danger. He believed that sex should be limited to monogamous marriages, but he did not oppose birth control.

He believed that homosexuality was wrong, but no more so than other sins. Therefore, he didn't believe that a homosexual man or woman should lose his or her civil rights any more than he believed that liars or drunkards should lose theirs. He believed that homosexuals should be allowed to teach in public schools as long as they didn't promote their lifestyle.

> *Dad was so convinced that truth could withstand scrutiny that he made sure students at Liberty were taught both the theory of evolution and creation. Christians are considered close-minded, yet none of the liberal universities who consider themselves open-minded teach both sides of that issue.*
>
> —JEANNIE FALWELL SAVAS

Jerry wanted children to be able to pray in schools, but he thought those prayers should be voluntary. He didn't believe that a school official should write a mandatory prayer, and he didn't believe that any child should be forced to participate in one.

Another lie some threw at Jerry was that he was a book burner. But in reality, Jerry hated censorship of any kind. He believed that truth could withstand scrutiny, so he brought speakers from both sides of every issue to speak at Liberty. He wanted the students to have their belief systems challenged.

The world's staggering number of nuclear arms was something else Jerry opposed, yet he believed the nation should maintain a strong national defense as a deterrent for war.

The Bible declares that any nation that helps Israel will be blessed. This was one of the reasons Jerry believed America should support them. But he also believed that we should work for peace in the Middle East and help all our Arab allies.

> *I took a class at Yale one summer, and my professor started talking about what Dad believed. Like most people, he was totally off-base. I finally interrupted and said, "That's not what he believes."*
>
> *"How would you know?" he asked with contempt.*
>
> *"I know because I'm his son."*
>
> —JERRY FALWELL JR.

He believed that America should do everything in its power to stop the flow of illegal drugs into the country, and he worked hard to change the laws so that children wouldn't see pornography in the aisles of grocery and convenient stores.

For the most part, Jerry ignored the smear campaign against him. Early in his ministry, one of his mentors, Dr. B. R. Lakin, said, "Jerry, your friends will know better, and your enemies will hate you anyway." Jerry took those words to heart. In addition, he'd stood firm in his convictions against his friends, colleagues, and mentors at Baptist Bible College when he was only twenty-two years old. Now he let the lies and innuendos roll off his back as he forged ahead to strengthen the Moral Majority and to work to get elected those officials who believed as he did on crucial moral issues.

Small-Town Preacher

The Moral Majority helped put President Reagan back in the White House for a second term. On January 21, 1985, Jerry and I stood outside in freezing temperatures for President Reagan's second inauguration. Although everyone was honored to attend, the wind chill was thirty-five degrees below zero, and most of us felt as though we would freeze into ice sculptures.

Due to the miserable weather, the outdoor ceremony was canceled, and we were among a small group invited inside the Rotunda to witness President Reagan's swearing-in. It was heartening to see elected officials take office who worked hard to defend moral values.

Jerry had committed five years to the Moral Majority, but he spent a total of eight years accomplishing his goals. During that time, we became friends with not only President and Mrs. Reagan, but President George H. W. Bush and President George W. Bush and their families. For a shy girl from Lynchburg who wanted nothing more than to stay out of the limelight, I was stunned to find myself invited to the White House on numerous occasions.

In addition to Presidents Reagan and Bush, we were privileged to meet President Ford and President Nixon. When I married that skinny young man who'd started Thomas Road Baptist Church in rural Virginia, I never imagined that one day he would be counted a friend of Menachem Begin, who presented Jerry with the Jabotinsky Award for his many years of faithful support to Israel. Nor did I dream that one day he would meet with King Hussein of Jordan, Anwar Sadat of Egypt, or Israeli prime ministers Benjamin Netanyahu and Shimon Peres. He met Yitzhak Rabin a mere eight weeks before his assassination.

> *We were having dinner with President George H. W. Bush at the White House when I had a startling revelation. The leader of the free world takes the dog out just like the rest of us.*
>
> —MACEL FALWELL

I thought I'd married a small-town Baptist preacher, but instead found myself playing the piano for one of the largest churches in America. More times than I can count, I have thanked God that He did not show me these events back then. He knew me well enough to be certain that I would have fled from our future and our destiny. But, while I looked forward to having my husband home when he finished what he was doing for the Moral Majority, I was so grateful that God had chosen us—ordinary, flawed people that we were—for just such a time as this in the history of this great nation.

CHAPTER SIX

Strength for the Journey

Elmer Towns stepped into Jerry's office and stopped cold. "What kind of stupid diet are you on?" he asked, staring at Jerry's gaunt frame.

Jerry shut the door to his office. "I'm not on a diet," he admitted. "I haven't eaten for twenty-five days. I'm on a forty-day fast, praying for a financial miracle."

"I'm sorry, Jerry. I'm so sorry," Elmer said, aware that Liberty University needed a financial infusion to satisfy its accrediting agency that the school had the necessary resources to fulfill its mission. Although Elmer had been the professor Jerry hired back in 1971 to start Liberty, not even he had known about Jerry's fast. At the time, only his family knew. While Jerry wasn't shy about public fund-raising for a worthy project, when he needed a miracle he didn't go on television.

He went to God.

This was his second forty-day fast in just a few months, and the one that took the greatest toll on his body. Dr. Towns, a prolific author, would later write a book based on Jerry's fasts. *Fasting for Spiritual Breakthrough: A Guide to Nine Biblical Feasts* became a classic on the subject. But at that moment, twenty-five days into his fast, Jerry felt as though he was a long way from breakthrough.

I found it interesting that Jerry's greatest battle hadn't been building Thomas Road Baptist Church. It hadn't been founding the Moral Majority or even the quagmire of stepping into the PTL scandal. The longest and fiercest battle he ever fought was establishing Liberty University.

A Man with a Mission

It all started about the time our son Jerry Jr. was going into first grade. Jerry was disturbed that Bible reading and prayer had been banned from public schools. One day in 1967, in the same tone in which one might say, "I'm going to the grocery store," Jerry announced, "I'm going to start a school."

"Jerry!" I said, stunned at the very idea. "You can't do that!"

I don't know if my reaction was prophetic insight or if I was just a doubting Thomas. It may have been a combination of the two.

But, of course, he did do it. That very year, using the facilities at Thomas Road, he began the Lynchburg Christian Academy. At first the school offered only kindergarten and first grade. But before long Jerry said, "I want to add second through fifth grades."

"Oh, Jerry, you just can't do that!" I said, still not grasping, even after all those years of marriage, that if Jerry and God hatched a plan they would accomplish it. Before I had time to eat my words the academy had grown to include kindergarten through fifth grades.

"I want to start a high school," Jerry announced one evening.

You'd think I would've learned to just agree with him by then, but I hadn't. "Jerry! You can't start a high school."

I might as well have waved a red flag in front of a bull as tell Jerry he couldn't do something. However, once the decision was made I always gave him my full support, even though his vision was far larger than anything I could have imagined. Once he made up his mind that God wanted him to do something—anything—it was a good idea to get out of his way.

A College to Change the World

I'll never forget the day we were driving across town and Jerry said, "I'm going to start a college."

"That's the most ridiculous thing I've ever heard," I said. "What do you know about starting a college?"

"Not much," he admitted, "but I'll learn."

"Besides, who would go to your college?"

From the backseat, five-year-old Jeannie piped up, "I will! I'll go to your college, Daddy!" That settled it. At that moment, Jerry would have built the college just for Jeannie.

While I certainly shivered at the overwhelming task of starting a college, none of us knew back then what it would eventually cost him.

Dr. Elmer Towns popped up on Jerry's radar screen when he wrote a bestselling book called *The Ten Largest Sunday Schools and What Makes Them Grow*. At the time, most people were opposed to big churches. It was popular to go to house churches and home churches, but Elmer's book broke that mind-set by studying ten huge churches that were nevertheless fundamentalist and didn't compromise on doctrinal issues. Not only were those churches thriving (not dying, as many people assumed) but they were traditional, soul-winning churches with altar calls in which many people were getting saved. Dr. Towns's book ranked Thomas Road Baptist Church as the ninth-largest Sunday school in the nation.

When Jerry sought advice about whom he should get to help him start a college, it was Elmer Towns's name that kept coming up. At the time Elmer was teaching at Trinity Evangelical Divinity School in Deerfield, Illinois. On the last weekend of January 1971, Elmer was preaching at Canton Baptist Temple in Canton, Ohio, which was one of the ten largest churches in America. That Saturday night, the pastor, Harold Henniger, looked across the supper table and said, "Elmer, you must go and start a college for Jerry Falwell."

"No," Elmer said, "I was there a couple of years ago and he only had up to the fifth grade. He said he was going to add a grade a year, so he won't be ready to start a college for five years."

"I know Jerry," Howard insisted. "He's impetuous, and he's going to start a college this summer. Tonight when you go back to your suite, call him."

"Okay, I'll do it," Elmer said in the same way someone might say, "Let's have lunch sometime."

When Howard dropped Elmer off at his room, he thumped on Elmer's chest with his finger. "I want you to call Jerry tonight! Will you promise me?"

"Yes, all right!" Elmer said.

Walking into the room and still wearing his coat, he picked up the phone and dialed our number.

Jerry answered, but he didn't bother with hello. He picked up the phone and said, "Elmer, what are we going to call the college?"

Elmer blinked several times, stunned. "Jerry, you don't talk about the name of a college. You talk about the purpose and what you want to accomplish. I'm an academic man, and we've got to start with the basics. Let me tell you what kind of college you want."

"What do I want?" Jerry asked, intrigued.

"You don't want just a Bible college," Elmer explained. "I know you. You want a college to train doctors, lawyers, businessmen, educators, pastors, and missionaries. What you want is a liberal arts college."

"Oh, no," Jerry said, laughing. "Don't call it *liberal*."

"Okay," Elmer said, "I won't call it 'liberal,' but there are three things you want in a college. The first thing you want is a college that's as academically respectable as any top-notch school but without their compromise on doctrine and standards."

"You're right," Jerry said.

"So the first thing you want is a college with academic excellence."

"I agree."

"Yours was the first church to use a computer, Jerry, so I know that the second thing you want is a college that's streamlined with cutting-edge technology."

"That's right," Jerry said, getting more excited by the moment.

"The third thing you want is a soul-winning college," Elmer said. "Something like Baptist Bible College in Springfield, but more upscale."

"Right again."

"On those three things will hinge all the decisions you make about this college you want to start. But I know your heart, Jerry, and I know you want to start a college that will change the world."

"That's exactly what I want!" Jerry said, stunned that Elmer read him so well.

"If I come and help you build this college, I'll write the constitution and it will be based on this premise: A Christian college is the extension of a local church at the collegiate level. If you listen to me, your college will change the world. All the other Christian colleges are interdenominational—think of Moody and Dallas Seminary. But your college will be controlled by a church. The college will be an extension of the ministry of the church.

"That means all of our students will be members of Thomas Road. They'll work in Christian service there. If they haven't been baptized they'll be baptized there. Our standards will be high, but they won't be legalistic. We'll expect from our students what we expect from Christians in a local church. We won't put any more or any less standards on our kids than that. How do you want the young people in a Christian church to live?"

"Boy, I love this! I *love* this!"

That settled, Elmer outlined all the courses they would offer. And then they discussed a name. "All the great colleges, like Wheaton and Georgetown, are named with geographic themes," Elmer explained. "Let's name it Lynchburg Baptist College."

Jerry and Elmer talked for an hour, setting up the curriculum. Afterward, Elmer realized that there was one major obstacle to his moving to Lynchburg and helping Jerry start a college, and that was Elmer's wife. Ruth, a powerful prayer warrior and intercessor, was settled into their home and might not like the idea of being uprooted. After hanging up with Jerry, Elmer breathed a prayer and phoned home.

"Oh, praise the Lord!" Ruth said when she heard her husband's voice. "I've been praying for an hour and fifteen minutes for you to call home."

"Why?" Elmer asked, "is something wrong?"

"Jerry Falwell called earlier," she explained, "and he wants you to come help him start a college." The hairs on Elmer's arms stood on end as he realized that while Howard Henniger had been pounding his chest and demanding that he phone Jerry, Jerry had been on the phone with Ruth.

Lord, what are you doing? Elmer thought as he listened to his wife.

Regardless of what was going on, Doc was just fun. He didn't like anything negative, and he talked every day with positive enthusiasm. When we were working or just driving home from a meeting, if there was a pause in the conversation Doc went into what I called his happy neutral and whistled. He wasn't negative about anything, and he never complained. He was one of the happiest and most joyful people I ever knew.

—DR. RON GODWIN

Ruth went on: "Jerry called and said, 'I don't usually talk to a man's wife about her husband coming to work for me, but do you think Elmer might?' I asked Jerry if he knew that you'd been a college president, and he didn't. I asked him if he knew that you'd been on an accreditation board, and he didn't. I promised that when I talked to you I'd have you call him.

"I heard enough about the college that I wanted to go there. But I knew that since it was an unknown school in an unknown city that you might turn it down. So I started praying, 'Lord, convince Elmer!' "

God did convince Elmer, and on June 4, 1971—only four months later—he and Ruth moved to Lynchburg.

Study Where Jesus Walked

Jerry and Elmer then faced a huge task: to raise enough money to start a college and to find students who would like to attend. When Elmer dropped his wife and children off at a motel and went to his first meeting, he was stunned to discover that Jerry had applications from only four potential students.

"Jerry," Elmer said, "I left a position in a well-recognized, up-and-coming school, and I'm going to be embarrassed if we only get fifty students. I don't want to teach at what people might call a two-bit college."

"Okay," Jerry said, "let's put an ad in the back of *Christianity Today* and all the top Christian magazines."

"You don't understand. Most magazines have already laid out their August issue at least. It's the middle of June, and if we get an ad to them by July first, it won't run until September, at the earliest."

"Then we'll have to build the college the way we built the church," Jerry said, meaning that they needed to think outside the box. "I'm going to Israel and a lot of pastors will go with me," Jerry continued. "Why don't I say that every pastor who sends us five students will get a free trip? Better yet, what if I give a free trip to a pastor who only gives me one student?"

"Jerry," Elmer said, a look of revelation on his face, "let's give the free trip to the *students.*"

"Let's do it!"

And so they offered students an academic tour, with a class in Israel. *If you come to our college you can study where Jesus walked,* they promised.

While launching their enrollment strategy, Jerry and Elmer also had to raise the funds to support a college. In order to get it off the ground, Jerry paid Elmer $200 a week totaling $10,400 a year. In order to draw a crowd and interest people in supporting the college, they paid Doug Oldham $1,000 a week. Doug put on gospel concerts, and afterward Jerry stood up and told the crowd about the college, asking people to help support it. At first, those who donated to the college were called *doorkeepers,* but they changed the term to *faith partners* and that's what they're still called today.

Elmer had just arrived in town when he and Jerry started trying to raise money for a college. Jerry and Elmer flew out to a Baptist church in western Virginia where about 250 people were gathered.

"Would you give a dollar a week to support this college?" Jerry asked. Jerry urged them to support their local church with their tithe, but if they could spare a little on top of that, perhaps it could come to one of our ministries, like the school. Those who were interested were given a packet with information and an envelope to mail in their gift. That summer Jerry and Elmer flew somewhere almost every evening to put on a concert and raise money for the college.

We had systems in place to log the money people sent. Every time we opened an envelope we took out a dollar and put it in the log book. But the IRS said we couldn't continue doing so. They said we had to write each person an individual receipt and mail it to them. By the time we wrote a receipt, put it in an envelope, and mailed it back, we ended up paying $1.07 for every dollar we received. So we stopped asking for the $1 offerings and went with $10. The following year we asked our faith partners for $15, and we've never gone beyond that amount.

Kids loved the idea of studying in Israel, and began flocking to enroll. In September 1971, with no buildings and using the church for space, we enrolled 154 students. That first day was exciting. For classes we used Sunday school classrooms, which were set up to handle sixty to seventy people. The church's library had a Dewey decimal system, so we used it. We used the gym and fed the students in the church cafeteria. We bought little houses across the street from the church and used them for dormitories. There were as many as nine students sharing one bathroom.

That first year we offered only

> *The greatness of what Macel Falwell did is what she didn't do. She didn't criticize. She supported Jerry. That first summer we were gone almost every evening, and she cheered us on.*
>
> —DR. ELMER TOWNS

> *I remember arriving at Thomas Road Baptist Church and asking where my dormitory was. I was led across the street to a little house. When I asked where my room was, a carpenter who was fixing a hole in the wall told me to pick any room I'd like. He told me the beds were out on the porch. There I found a stack of bunk beds and mattresses. I picked out a room and set up my bed, and began the most exciting, rewarding days of my life.*
>
> —STEVE VANDEGRIFF, LBC GRADUATE, 1975; SEMINARY GRADUATE, 1977

a freshman curriculum. The second year we offered freshman and sophomore curricula, adding instructors and courses each year.

Finding the Faculty

At the time, the church was running a steady three thousand in attendance, with another couple of thousand showing up for special events. Dr. Pierre Guillermin, a graduate of Bob Jones University, had started our academy, which now included kindergarten through grade twelve. A former college president, Dr. Guillermin taught at the college, as did Dr. Towns. Elmer found two other former college presidents, one from a Presbyterian college and the other from a Southern Baptist college. Our struggling little college had four former college presidents on its faculty.

Elmer had served on the board of the Accrediting Association of Bible Colleges. This helped him as he began negotiations with the State of Virginia to get us certified by the state Department of

Education. He also flew to Atlanta to talk to people there about our being accredited by the Southern Association of Colleges and Schools.

It was hard to build a college up from nothing, and a college without a history is difficult to run. They had to stay one event ahead of the students all the time, because, without a history, there was no built-in loyalty. There were also no upperclassmen teaching the younger students.

Halfway through that first year, Elmer hired Greg Lampe, a young man with a Ph.D. in biology, as registrar. Just before the end of that first year, he hired Dr. J. Gordon Henry, who had a Ph.D. from the University of Kentucky, to be academic dean. Elmer himself stepped into the role of executive vice president. From the very beginning, they hired as many faculty members with Ph.D.s as possible.

I Want That Mountain

Jerry's little college wasn't even accredited yet, and with only 154 students it was far from impressive. Yet the vision God had given him for the college rivaled Notre Dame and Brigham Young. Jerry imagined a future in which the university would have fifty thousand students. He knew there was only one place near Lynchburg that could accommodate such a campus.

Candler's Mountain.

One afternoon as Jerry winged his way home, he looked out the window of the airplane and remembered sitting on that very mountain as a child and knowing that one day he would own it.

I was fifteen years old when I moved to Lynchburg to attend the academy and then Liberty. I didn't know a soul when I arrived, but a few weeks later I was up at bat during a ball game when I heard this unmistakable voice shout, "Come on, Big John!" I froze. How does Jerry Falwell know my name?

—JOHN BARRICK, LIBERTY UNIVERSITY ALUMNUS;
JERRY FALWELL'S DENTIST

Jerry turned to his friend William H. Burruss Jr., and asked if he knew who owned the land.

William didn't know, but they later found out. They found that 2,100 acres of the mountain was owned by United States Gypsum Company.

Jerry flew to Chicago to meet with a vice president of the company. "Is there any way you'll sell that land?"

"Strange that you should ask that question," the man told Jerry. "Just days ago we decided to sell the exact parcel of land you're asking about."

The asking price was $1,250,000. United States Gypsum needed cash, and Jerry didn't have any. But what he had was better than gold—he had a dream, and the faith that God would bring it to pass.

"We'll take it," Jerry said. "Would you consider financing it?"

The man laughed as he shook his head.

"Could you give me a ninety-day option so that we can raise some money?" Jerry asked.

"Yes," the man said, "but you'll need to leave some earnest

money." He was thinking about Jerry's offering $100,000 in earnest money for more than a million-dollar selling price.

"How about ten thousand dollars?" Jerry asked.

Laughing harder now, the man said, "Can you get ninety thousand to go with it in thirty days?"

"I can," Jerry answered.

"Then it's yours."

Jerry gave him a check for $10,000 and, on his way out the door, said, "By the way, don't cash the check for a few days. We don't have *any* money, but we'll get it."

And get it he did. People across the country sent donations and pledges and we borrowed the rest.

The Great Awakening

In order to draw more students, the second year we offered them a free trip to England to study the Great Awakening. They would visit the home of John Wesley and the site where George Whitfield preached. We started the second year with 22 full-time faculty members and 420 students.

How do you get 420 students to England? The charter company flew one planeload of students over, and then it flew back to the United States, where the pilot slept before taking the next load. One group started on the East Coast and another on the West Coast, and they met somewhere in between.

The kids stayed in bed-and-breakfasts, hostels, and in people's homes. They slept three to a double bed with two on the floor. In Stratford-upon-Avon, Elmer's daughter ended up sleeping upstairs over a bar that had been frequented by William Shakespeare. They visited Shakespeare's house and Oxford. To hold their lectures, they rented huge churches for only $25.

They made learning come alive.

Back home in Lynchburg we had to find room for the new college's ever-expanding student body. As the school grew, we bought the old Virginian Hotel downtown and renovated six floors to house four hundred students. Other students lived at the Kennedy House, an abandoned hospital, and we rented out a floor of the old Ramada Inn. We were housing them in campsites on Treasure Island and old, unheated buses transported them to their classes, meals, and chapel services.

> If America is to remain free, we must raise up a generation of young people who are trained as witnesses for Christ and voices for righteousness who can call this nation back to God and back to the principles upon which it was built. We must bring America back to God and back to greatness. We can only do it by helping young people find purpose in life in Christ.
>
> —JERRY FALWELL

For a while, our only school sport was basketball, and almost every male on campus played on the team. Jerry often ducked in to practice with them.

It's All in the Name

We were into our fourth year when a woman sent a $100,000 check made out to Lynchburg College, intending it to go to our school. After a month, she called and asked why Jerry never acknowledged the gift or sent a receipt. Jerry talked to her and said, "That would be the greatest gift, but we never received it."

We'd named our school Lynchburg Baptist College. Unfortunately for us, only three blocks away was another school called Lynchburg College. The woman had made her check out to Lynchburg College and it had been sent to the other school and deposited into their account. Jerry talked to the president of Lynchburg College and they gave us the $100,000.

Neither Jerry nor Elmer ever wanted that mistake to happen again, so the college was renamed Liberty Baptist College.

Next was the formation of a seminary. In total, then, Jerry's educational program could take a child from kindergarten all the way through postgraduate work.

In 1976, the fall semester saw 1,871 students starting classes. Many of the students slept on the floor until space could be arranged for them. The student body now represented forty-nine states and ten foreign countries. That same year, Liberty Baptist Theological Seminary graduated its first class.

Taking the Mountain by Faith

In January 1977 temperatures plummeted to the single digits as students sat in classes at the old Brookville High School, shivering in their coats and gloves. The abandoned school was scheduled to be torn down, but for now we needed the space. Heaters were rented to try to warm the building, but they took oxygen out of the air and made the students lightheaded.

Distressed because he had nowhere else to take the kids, Jerry spent the whole bleak night praying for an answer. Over the next few days he looked high and low for rental property that would get the kids out of that building, but could find none.

When Jerry couldn't find a spiritual breakthrough in prayer alone, he believed in calling in the troops. On January 21, a group of 2,500 students, faculty, and administration tramped through eight inches of snow for an open-air prayer meeting on Liberty Mountain (Candler's Mountain). They sang "I Want That Mountain" and asked God for the finances to let them start building classrooms that could be used in the fall.

They prayed for almost two hours, making no provision for defeat. The following month, in February, the school received financial gifts totaling more than $2.5 million. On March 1, we launched a building program on Liberty Mountain. By the fall of 1977, students were attending classes in brand-new buildings on that mountain.

On March 30, 1979, two years after that prayer time, we trekked back up the mountain to dedicate the 3,000-square-foot multipurpose center, which would provide space for classes, chapel, and sporting events. By the end of the year, twenty-one buildings were in some stage of completion on Liberty Mountain.

> *Jerry has the ability to say what he wants and get what he says.*
> —DR. ELMER TOWNS

How Great the Fall

The primary source of Liberty's income came from Jerry's television ministry. As Liberty took its first toddling steps as a young college, we had no idea that we could lose that income overnight.

In 1987, scandal wrapped itself around Jim Bakker and PTL, with the Jimmy Swaggart scandal not far behind. As those ministers fell, all televangelists were judged guilty by association. Almost overnight, Liberty lost millions of dollars in financial support.

Although Liberty's expenses multiplied with the enrollment, our income shrank to a dribble by comparison. Before the ink was dry on the tabloids, we were $82 million deep in short-term debt. We went from a college being supported by television to one staggering under a massive burden of debt. If Liberty didn't learn to support itself, she would drown in it.

Jerry Jr. had recently graduated from law school—just in time to step up and help Jerry. The two of them sheltered the rest of the family from the severity of the situation as much as possible.

In addition to lost income, Jerry had too many students on scholarship. There weren't enough students paying tuition for the school to support itself. The struggle to make payroll each payday seemed overwhelming, and the faculty stood staunch at Jerry's side through a couple of payless paydays.

> *It is not the mountains ahead of us which wear us down. It is often the grain of sand in our shoe. God never puts more on us than He puts in us to bear up every burden.*
>
> —JERRY FALWELL

Another strong ally through the years has been Dr. Ron Godwin. He'd come to Liberty's faculty with a Ph.D. in planning and management. "One day we needed $250,000 to make payroll," Dr. Godwin recalls. "Two hours before the close of business that day, Dr. Falwell walked into my office and said, 'When are we ever going to learn?'

" 'Learn what?' I asked.

" 'I just got a wire for $300,000. When are we ever going to learn that the Lord knows what He's doing?' "

Yet even while staggering under millions of dollars of debt, old habits were hard to break. "Jerry had one ability that far exceeded his ability to raise money, and that was to give it away," Dr. Godwin explains. "While we were struggling financially, if Doc was going out to eat with a pastor, one of us always went with him, because if we didn't he would buy the guy a new church parking lot.

"Money was just something to be used for God. He really didn't think about it much. Periodically I'd tell him to empty his pockets. Sure enough, there would be checks he'd been carrying around for weeks and had forgotten to deposit."

> *I had many sleepless nights, but it didn't bother Dad as much. He seemed oblivious to the wolves at the door.*
> —JERRY FALWELL JR.

In 1981, the year Liberty celebrated its tenth anniversary, we were accepted into the National Collegiate Athletic Association (NCAA) Division II. A month later, our wrestling team placed first in the NAIA district tournament.

Yet, as the student body continued to multiply, so did the need for classrooms and dormitories. That meant it took more and more money to support the college. We were outgrowing our eighteen dormitories, four classroom buildings, administration building, prayer chapel, and 4,000-seat multipurpose center.

It took great faith to keep Liberty going, but it also took a tremendous amount of money, which was in very short supply.

The Best of Times, The Worst of Times

God directed Jerry to cut back on some of his political work, because Liberty University would need all of his spiritual and physical strength to survive.

While the financial outlook appeared grim, there were high points along the way. For instance, in 1990 the Pittsburgh Steelers picked Eric Green, one of our football players, as a first-round NFL draft choice. And on May 12, 1990, President George H. W. Bush, along with his wife, Barbara, flew to Roanoke and then boarded the Marine One helicopter to head to Lynchburg. President Bush came to Liberty to give the commencement address before a crowd of sixteen thousand.

Jerry believed Liberty had passed a huge financial hurdle later that year when a company in Chicago agreed to fund a multimillion-dollar bond issue that would stop the hemorrhage. In November, only days before Liberty's debt was to be paid off, the company backed out of its agreement.

"The two worst days in Dad's life," Jerry Jr. explains, "were the day in 1977 when his mother died and the day the Chicago-based company failed to keep their commitment. He looked destroyed. Their reneging on the deal caused all of Liberty's short-term debt to be in default. We spent all of 1991 trying to find long-term financing, but were unsuccessful."

Liberty University was in such dire financial straits that many people predicted that it would be forced to close. All construction on the new dining hall stopped, leaving an unfinished shell. Once again, students, faculty, and administrative staff prayed and fasted.

In the spring of 1992, we all circled the unfinished building and asked God for the finances to complete it. Two local businessmen, Dan Reber and Jimmy Thomas, stepped forward with money to finish the building. On the first day of fall classes, the same group gathered around the completed cafeteria and thanked God.

Liberty Defies the Odds

On February 24, 1993, headlines in the Lynchburg *News & Advance* read, Liberty Defies Odds, Survives Turmoil. Only God could have kept us afloat through those troubling times.

The following month, as though God were giving His stamp of approval, Liberty received initial accreditation of its nursing program. In May, Senator Jesse Helms gave the commencement address. That fall, God answered our prayers, not with money, but with His presence. Revival swept across the campus. Entire dormitories fasted and prayed as students gave their hearts to the Lord, committed to full-time service, and rededicated their lives to God. As the wind of God's Spirit blew across campus, it revived us and gave us strength for the journey still ahead.

In spite of staggering debt, the university kept growing. By 1996, Liberty had 5,500 resident students who lived, prayed, and studied on the $200 million campus, which was spread over 3,000 acres. On our twenty-fifth anniversary, Jerry was heartened to learn that over 700 of our graduates were serving overseas as missionaries, 25,000 alumni were serving in various vocations worldwide, 1,200 were senior pastors, and hundreds more were serving as associate pastors, youth pastors, or as church staff.

Through prayer and hard work the dream that Jerry and Elmer Towns dared to believe in was coming to pass. They had built a university that was changing the world. Even so, ten years after the fall of Jim Bakker and Jimmy Swaggart, Liberty had yet to dig its way out of the financial quagmire those ministries had left in their wake.

One way God gave Jerry strength for the journey was by directing Jerry Jr. to get a law degree and calling him to work alongside Jerry. Both of them believed Romans 8:28: "And we know that all things work together for good to those who love God, to those who are the called according to His purpose."

As difficult as it was to keep up with the financial needs of a university growing at warp speed, both Jerry and Jerry Jr. believed that, in the long run, being forced to make the transition from being supported by television to supporting itself would be a blessing, something that would leave Liberty in much better shape for the next generation.

Liberty was in a constant state of construction and expansion—because every year the enrollment took another leap. New dormitories, new classrooms, new technology, and new faculty required a lot of money, making it difficult to whittle away too much of the existing debt. We seemed to be playing a constant game of catch-up.

In 1996, the accrediting agency demanded more improvement. If we didn't reduce the debt to $20 million, they said, we were in danger of losing our accreditation. Desperate for a breakthrough, Jerry embarked on two forty-day fasts.

That's when Dr. Elmer Towns came in and uttered his famous words, "What kind of stupid diet are you on?" and Jerry admitted that he was twenty-five days into a forty-day fast to raise the millions of dollars that were needed.

People who don't understand the principle of fasting might think it a strange thing for Jerry to give up solid foods and live only on liquids, but the Bible is filled with examples of people in crisis situations who needed a miracle and sought God by humbling themselves through prayer and fasting.

Perhaps fasting works because the first sin in the Garden of Eden involved *not* denying ourselves of food. Adam and Eve ate the forbidden food, and this brought a curse. Maybe that's why going without food for spiritual purposes seems to bring God's blessing.

At this point Jerry was desperate for God's blessing on Liberty University. He still believed in the vision of a college that would change the world as much as he had back in 1971, when he and Elmer flew from town to town asking people to send a dollar a week to support it. Only now—twenty-six years later—it took a lot of dollars to keep it going and keep it growing.

So Jerry had launched his second forty-day fast that year, asking God for a financial miracle. As the fast progressed, people wondered at Jerry's loss of weight and gaunt features. Finally, he announced his fast from the pulpit, and some of our members picked up the burden to pray.

This Is the Confidence

Although I did not go on a forty-day fast with Jerry, I was nevertheless relieved as the final day drew to a close. From outward appearances, the fast did not seem to have changed a thing—except Jerry's weight. The debt Liberty owed still blinked from the computer screen as though to mock his efforts. But Jerry, ever the optimist, believed that God had heard him.

For Jerry, the matter was simple. First John 5:14–15 says: "Now this is the confidence that we have in Him, that if we ask anything according to His will, He hears us. And if we know that He hears us, whatever we ask, we know that we have the petitions that we have asked of Him."

Jerry knew that he had prayed and humbled himself before the Lord. He knew that when he prayed, God listened and heard him. And according to 1 John 5:14–15, if God heard him, then he *already* had the answer in the realm of the Spirit, and it would be manifest in the natural realm in time.

While people who don't understand spiritual principles might laugh at that kind of simplicity, Jerry didn't care. He woke every morning thanking God for the answer and, having done all he could do, he refused to fret about the situation. While others might worry about how they were going to make the next payroll, Jerry believed he would get the full amount that he'd asked God to provide.

As it turned out, he didn't have long to wait.

"Elmer, come here, I want to show you something," Jerry said.

"What is it?" Dr. Towns asked.

"There's a courier flying in with a check for me from A. L. Williams," Jerry explained, grinning. A. L. Williams is a businessman who believes deeply in the vision of Liberty University. Soon afterward, a man arrived and handed Jerry confirmation of a wire transfer in the amount of $27 million.

"Look at this!" Jerry said, holding up the check.

"Let me touch it!" Elmer responded.

"Nobody touches this," he said, laughing.

"That's staggering," Elmer said as the two men stared in awe.

It was an astonishing demonstration of God's faithfulness to answer prayer.

"Jerry," Elmer Towns said, as the two men worked to secure Liberty's future, "that second forty-day fast almost ruined your health."

"I was doing it to save the school, Elmer. You know, you can only die once. I'd do it again to save Liberty."

> The greatest thing about Jerry Falwell was his faith. I think his faith was greater than his ability to preach, to manage, or to administer. He just believed God.
> —DR. ELMER TOWNS

The preceding May, Billy Graham had delivered the commencement address at Liberty University. Afterward he handed a diploma to his grandson, William Franklin Graham IV, while his son William Franklin Graham III, looked on. Liberty University was no longer a campus without a history. Its history had become rich and its future beamed like a beacon to the world.

CHAPTER SEVEN

My Enemies, My Friends

The sun set over Smith Mountain Lake in a spectacular blaze of crimson as we finished dinner and settled down for a quiet evening of board games and reading. It was the summer of 1987 and we'd escaped to our lake house so Jerry could rest and get recharged. Jerry dropped into his favorite chair and sighed with contentment.

Only moments later, the shrill ringing of the telephone shattered the silence. Jerry answered. I watched his jovial face turn serious as he hung up the phone.

"FBI agents are on their way here," he said. "There's something they want to discuss with us."

The FBI? My nerves stood on end as we waited their arrival. *What now?*

The men stepped inside and got straight to the point. "I'm

sorry to tell you this," one man said, "but we've uncovered a kidnapping plot, and your daughter, Jeannie, is the target."

Jeannie! My hands flew to my face as I tried to still my racing heart and listen. Jeannie, in her second year of medical school, lived in Richmond. I knew without asking that she wouldn't consider taking a sabbatical in order to wait until the kidnapper was caught.

The FBI explained their plan to us. In an attempt to keep her safe and also to apprehend the man behind the scheme, the FBI would set up surveillance in an apartment near Jeannie's.

The days and weeks that followed were tense and filled with suspense. It was difficult for us to go about our normal routine, and I have no idea how Jeannie handled the stress of medical school while knowing she'd been targeted for a crime. After a few weeks the man was apprehended, and to this day we aren't sure if he was all talk or if he would have carried out his threat.

This kidnapping plot hit us so hard because it involved our only daughter, but it was hardly the first incident of its kind. It joined a long line of death threats, bomb threats, and attacks we had suffered due to Jerry's involvement with the Moral Majority. What happened to due process? Call me naïve, but what happened to being innocent until proven guilty?

Jerry's only crime had been mobilizing millions of Americans to exercise their right to vote. In days gone by, there had been opposition to allowing women to vote. Now the outpouring of hate, slurs, and violence let us know that there was a segment of society who wanted conservative voters to remain silent, without a voice in the government. In spite of the threats, Jerry refused to back down. So did Jeannie and so did the rest of our family.

Bomb Threat

When Jerry preached at Thomas Road Baptist Church he did so behind a bulletproof pulpit. He'd been such a lightning rod for controversy for years that the church's leadership insisted he take this and other precautions. For instance, he never checked into a hotel under his own name and he traveled with a security guard.

On one occasion, we'd invited Anita Bryant to Thomas Road. Jerry stood in the pulpit speaking to a packed house when someone from security walked across the stage and whispered in his ear.

"We've had a report that there's a bomb under the stage."

Jerry nodded his thanks to the man and turned back to his beloved congregation. "There's been a bomb threat."

What happened wasn't as significant as what *didn't* happen. Silence fell over the sanctuary. No one moved. People didn't jump over one another to fight their way toward an exit. Not a single person left the building.

"If you feel at all uneasy or frightened, please leave," Jerry urged. "But . . . I'm staying."

No one left.

Nor did a bomb go off.

Over the years members of the church let Jerry know in hundreds of ways that they would stand with him through good times and bad. But despite their loyalty and love, there was a growing tide of people who assaulted our house with eggs, put firecrackers in our mailbox, or called to threaten our family.

In 1979, as the situation began to spin out of control, it became obvious to Jerry and me that we had to find a more secluded place to raise our children. I found a historic plantation house sitting on seven acres, only seven minutes from the church.

On the Home Front

The house, built in 1849, was in sad shape, but the wooden-peg hardwood floors, tall windows, and beamed ceilings gave me confidence that with hard work and tender care it could live again. The asking price of $160,000 was more than we could afford, but Claude Brown, one of our friends and trustees, bought the house and gave it to the church. Later, Jerry and I purchased the home from the church.

Because of continued threats against our lives, the board financed the construction of an eight-foot security fence around the entire property. With an automatic gate and around-the-clock guards, we'd done all we knew how to do to protect our family.

As the house and grounds took shape, Jerry enjoyed praying under the old white oak trees that shaded the property and sheltered a small army of squirrels. One of our security guards found a baby squirrel almost dead in the frigid winter wind. After being nursed back to health, Max the squirrel took up residence near our back door. Whenever Max saw Jerry come home, he'd rush across the lawn, run up his pant legs, and perch, chattering, on his shoulder.

However, not even eight-foot walls, security guards, or a pet squirrel could keep danger from lurking at our door.

Late one night, Jerry was out of town as I puttered around the kitchen and watched television without the slightest sense of danger. Neither the security guard nor I had any idea that an intruder had scaled the wall. As I watched late-night programming, the guard made his rounds patrolling the property. The intruder jumped him from behind and threw him against a car. The two men struggled until the security guard got free. He burst into the house to verify that I was safe. Then he bellowed, "Lock yourself inside!"

I dashed to an interior bathroom, where I had often waited out storms. Trembling, I locked myself inside. By the time the security guard got back outside the man who'd attacked him had fled. He was never apprehended.

These were the unpleasant realities that we faced on a regular basis. They were small acts of terrorism, designed to intimidate and control us with fear. As frightening as those violent, unseen enemies were to me, their actions only cemented my resolve that Jerry should continue his work with the Moral Majority.

Over the Top

Most of the time Jerry didn't bother trying to defend himself against the onslaught of criticism that his opponents brought against him. Only when the attacks lapped over onto other people he loved and respected did he ever fight back.

For instance, his critics labeled him anti-Semitic because he visited both Anwar Sadat of Egypt and King Hussein of Jordan. They ignored the fact that he visited Israel more than twenty-five times and met with numerous prime ministers, including

Menachem Begin, who had presented Jerry with one of Israel's most coveted awards for his friendship with Israel. Yet why confuse their smear campaign with the truth?

Things heated up when the Carter-Mondale campaign announced on television that "Dr. Jerry Falwell says that God doesn't answer the prayers of the Jews." Jerry had never said that or anything like it. They went on to warn that if Ronald Reagan was elected president he would take Jerry with him and the two of them would "purify the land."

Those lies went over the top as far as Jerry was concerned, and the Moral Majority filed an $11 million lawsuit to stop the slander. The Carter-Mondale campaign knew they couldn't support their claims and they pulled the commercials. When they did, Jerry withdrew the lawsuit.

It didn't matter if the attacks came from national media, political enemies, or someone in the neighborhood, Jerry's response was generally the same. He had the uncanny ability to make friends of his enemies.

Brenda Phelps grew up down the street from the Donald Duck Bottling Company. "After Jerry Falwell started a church in the old Donald Duck building, our lives changed," Brenda recalls. "Back

---

I didn't take the slander against my dad personally because I knew he wasn't mean-spirited or judgmental. I also understood that Dad was just the messenger; the attacks were really aimed at God. However, I had naïvely believed that people wouldn't put things in print that weren't true.

—JEANNIE FALWELL SAVAS

then, my daddy was an alcoholic. As the church grew, parking became a problem. Daddy got so frustrated because people started parking in front of our house. He didn't like Jerry or what he stood for.

"One Sunday he took all the chairs from the kitchen table and sat them in the street so that no one could park there. I begged him not to do it, but to my embarrassment he did it Sunday after Sunday. One day Daddy ran into Jerry, and told him off. He said that Jerry might get all of Lynchburg in his church but he would never get him.

"Years later, Daddy got caught driving under the influence. When my sister and I went to pick him up at the police station, he was crying and calling for God to help him. That night Daddy asked Jesus into his heart. The next morning he went to see Jerry. The following Sunday, Jerry baptized Daddy and reminded him of what he'd said about never attending Jerry's church. Jerry and Daddy became friends, and Daddy became an usher."

I suspect that when Jerry ran across people like that, people who acted like a bear with a thorn, it reminded him of his father. He realized that they were acting from some deep wound in their own lives. As a result, Jerry responded with kindness, never held a grudge, and prayed.

The Odd Couple

The key to having friends is being one, and Jerry knew how to be a friend. One thing that surprised people about Jerry was that he didn't see any reason for opposing beliefs to be a barrier to friendship. Jerry respected other people's right to believe as they did, even if he didn't agree with them. That's why, when Jerry and Ted Kennedy became friends, the press labeled them the "Odd Couple."

In the fall of 1983, Senator Kennedy accepted an invitation to speak at Liberty University. "Most of you probably think it's easier for a camel to pass through the eye of a needle than for Ted Kennedy to speak at Liberty University," he began as four thousand students laughed and listened with respect to what he said. He ended his speech by promising to watch the *Old Time Gospel Hour* if Jerry would extend the students' curfew for an hour that night. Ted later said that he'd expected the Liberty students to boo, hiss, and disrupt his speech. He'd been pleased at their attention and respectful attitude.

That night, Ted Kennedy, his sister, Jean Smith, and his daughter, Kara, had dinner in our home with Jerry, me, and our three children. We spent a delightful evening together, even discussing our opposing beliefs, and each family listened to the other with interest and courtesy. Differences aside, we all loved our country and wanted to do our best to help find solutions to the problems we faced as a nation.

Several years later, we were invited to the Kennedys' home for dinner. I'll admit to being nervous about what we would be served, as I've never enjoyed fancy sauces or certain types of spicy foods. When we sat down to eat, I looked at the steak and baked potato on my plate with delight and thought, *They're just regular people!*

On a trip to Palm Beach, Jerry visited with Senator Kennedy again. The two men discussed their thoughts and feelings about the problems facing America. Before he left, Jerry prayed with Ted's mother, Rose, who was ill. When Jerry Jr. applied to law school, Ted Kennedy sent a glowing letter of recommendation. Then, in 1984, Jerry asked Senator Kennedy to join him in a debate at the National Religious Broadcasters convention. Both liberals and conservatives criticized the two men for their friendship, but Jerry believed that bridging those barriers was an important step to healing the nation. Besides, Jerry liked and respected Ted Kennedy.

Ted wasn't the only liberal who was kind to us. On one occasion Jerry and I were invited to have dinner at the home of Nelson Bunker Hunt, an oil company executive and son of H. L. Hunt, an American oil tycoon. Our driver dropped us off at a large and impressive home in the Dallas area. I thought I caught a flicker of surprise when a lady opened the front door to us and said, "*Reverend Falwell!* Oh . . . won't you come in?"

My first wrinkle of worry occurred when I noticed that the dining room table wasn't set. *How strange.* We were ushered to a beautiful room and offered something to drink.

"A Dr Pepper would be wonderful," Jerry said, and the woman left to get it.

"Jerry, I've got the funniest feeling that we're in the wrong place," I whispered.

"Oh, no," Jerry assured me, "our driver knew where he was going."

A few minutes later, the woman's husband arrived and we had a long and interesting conversation. With each passing moment I felt more uneasy. The dining table still wasn't set and I didn't smell any food cooking.

After a while, Jerry said, "Excuse me, but where's Bunker?"

"Bunker?" the man asked.

"Yes," Jerry said, waiting.

"Bunker . . . who?" the man asked, confused.

"Are we at the wrong place?" Jerry asked as his eyebrows rose almost to his hairline.

"Yes," the man said with a look of vast relief, "but we've so enjoyed talking to you."

Jerry explained to the couple that we'd been invited to the home of Bunker Hunt for dinner and that our driver had dropped us at this address. The man didn't know Bunker, and when he checked the phone directory he found that his address and phone were unlisted. Still, our gracious host called friends until he found the right address and drove us there himself. We later learned that our surprised host was on the opposite side of our political fence, but no one could have been more gracious.

The Power of Unity

By 1980, Jerry was receiving death threats on a daily basis. If he had any question about what lay at the root of them, that question was forever settled when he arrived in Madison, Wisconsin, for an *I Love America!* rally. During the concert, a group of demonstrators began their loud chant.

"Damn Jesus Christ! Damn Jesus Christ!"

Jerry tried to pray but the chanting and obscenities overwhelmed the sound system. Without warning, hundreds of protestors locked arms and moved like an advancing army against the crowd. People screamed as they fled the scene, elbowing and clawing their way to safety. No one could hear Jerry above the din.

"Preacher!" a pastor in the crowd shouted. "Don't worry—we can take care of them!"

The man locked arms with pastors on either side of him, and without another word, hundreds of pastors from across Wisconsin linked arms. Then, as one, they turned to face the screaming protestors, who shook their fists as they marched. The university choir continued to sing as the two groups met. Pastors and protestors looked one another in the eye in a standoff. Nobody moved as Jerry gave his speech. Afterward, security whisked him away.

"Those preachers stood up to the punks!" one of the policemen said in awe. "Who would have expected that from a bunch of preachers?"

Who indeed? In America, men and women of God had not been forced to lay their lives on the line as Christians had in other countries, so no one knew if they had any courage. But those pastors showed that they did. They were enraged by the chanting of the godless protestors. If Christians in this country would not unite against those who dared shout against Jesus, then we had already lost the most important battle of all.

Thank God, they did.

Bastions of Liberalism

Nowhere was liberalism more prevalent in those days than on the campuses of Harvard, Princeton, Berkeley, and Yale. And yet each of these institutions invited Jerry, then the leader of the Moral Majority, to speak on their campuses.

Those were not peaceful scenes, however. At Princeton a bomb threat forced the evacuation of a building just before Jerry spoke. At Yale University, as Jerry spoke students took up the chant, *"Hitler rose; Hitler fell. Racist Falwell, go to hell!"*

"Hitler rose; Hitler fell. Racist Falwell, go to hell!"

"Are you a racist?" one of the students asked after some of the loudest demonstrators had been removed.

> *Those students weren't to blame for their bad manners. In the media I had been compared to Ayatollah Khomeini, Adolf Hitler, and Jim Jones. They said I was sexist, racist, and anti-Semitic. If I believed what they had heard about me, I would have protested myself.*
>
> —JERRY FALWELL

"I was at one time," Jerry said into the microphone, "but most of what you've heard about me is untrue."

"Then why don't you have any black members in your church?"

"That's exactly what I'm talking about. You've been misinformed. We do have black members at Thomas Road Baptist Church. In fact, we have over four hundred members of ethnic minorities, and eleven percent of the students at Liberty University are minorities. Now, let me ask you a question. How many black students, professors, or administrators do you have at Yale?"

Silence followed his question. Jerry looked out over a sea of white faces, and the students looked around and saw the same thing: white students, white faculty, and white administrators. When the meeting was over, some of the students applauded and others reached out to shake Jerry's hand.

Sister Boom-Boom and the Press

The scene that met Jerry and Jonathan when they arrived in San Francisco in the summer of 1984 was chilling. When news of Jerry's arrival hit the press, thousands of violent protestors surrounded the hotel where he was scheduled to speak.

Riot police tried to control the mob as they hanged and then burned an effigy of President Reagan. An effigy of Jerry hung nearby. Transvestites wearing heavy makeup and dressed like nuns carried signs calling themselves Sister Boom-Boom and the Sisters of Perpetual Indulgence. More than a thousand demonstrators protested in a frenzy for two days, during which time Jonathan, disguised as a member of the press, took hundreds of astounding photographs and recorded what the protestors were saying.

As the situation heated up, police insisted that Jerry be moved in secret to another location. When the police started making arrests, Jonathan jumped in the back of a police vehicle with some of the radicals headed toward jail. Believing Jonathan to be a member of the press, one of the men said, "Falwell hates all homosexuals! He wants to deny us our civil rights. He doesn't want to allow us to teach in public schools. He wants us registered, monitored, and deported or placed in camps!"

Jonathan, shocked by the allegations, tried to explain Jerry's position.

> *One of the most important lessons those students needed to learn was that they were in danger of being misinformed and misled by television, radio, the press, and by their own professors even in this great nation of ours.*
>
> —JERRY FALWELL

At the time, Jerry had no idea what Jonathan was doing. Later, he walked into a television studio, where Sister Boom-Boom was waiting to be interviewed. Jonathan sat nearby wearing ragged jeans and a press pass. As Jerry shook Boom-Boom's hand, Jonathan said, "Hi, Dad." Boom-Boom appeared startled as Jerry turned and made the introduction, "I would like you to meet my son Jonathan."

When Jerry got home from that trip, he told me that that moment was forever frozen in his mind because as he looked at those two young men, Jonathan and Sister Boom-Boom, he loved them both so much that he wanted to hug them. He loved the fact that they were both willing to risk their lives for what they believed. He loved their zeal and their passion. What Sister Boom-Boom couldn't grasp was that while Jerry hated the sin of homosexuality, he never hated the sinner.

When Jerry and I looked through the vast array of photographs Jonathan took during those tumultuous days, our reactions said everything there was to say about our differences. Jerry was delighted with Jonathan's daring. I was unhappy because he'd put himself in danger.

Acting Up

That would not be the last time Jonathan put himself in harm's way in an effort to help his father. Much later, in 1992, four of us—Jonathan, Mark DeMoss, Duke Westover, and I—traveled with Jerry to Houston, where he was to speak at the Republican National Convention.

In a hotel down the street from the convention a militant group of homosexuals, calling themselves the AIDS Coalition to Unleash Power (ACT UP), were acting up about Jerry's presence in Houston. This was a group of very angry people. They'd been known to throw balloons filled with blood. Here, they mobbed the front of the hotel with signs denouncing Jerry.

The searing Texas sun steamed the parking lot as police and security guards rushed us through the back door. Inside, Duke waited near the stage with Jerry while Mark and I stood in the back. Jonathan slipped into a chair near the front of the audience. Police took up key positions, unaware that some of the demonstrators had gotten past security and into the room.

The audience seemed attentive as Jerry spoke—until the ear-splitting sound of an air horn blasted high and shrill from the far side of the room, drowning out everything else.

Everyone in the place, including the police, turned in unison to the sound. Even the policeman standing on the stage looked away. At that instant, with everyone turned toward the noise, two men jumped out of their seats and rushed toward Jerry.

The only person who recognized the ploy was Jonathan. He sprang from his seat, his lanky legs chewing up the distance before he took a flying leap and attacked both of the men from behind. Once he had them on the floor, he raced to the stage and yanked a policeman to Jerry's side.

It happened so fast—the horrific noise, the men rushing Jerry, chairs flying, and the determined blur of my youngest son protecting his father. Jerry survived the incident unharmed, but Jonathan suffered cuts and bruises to his hands and legs.

Jerry refused to let the escalating attacks deter him. Instead, he chose to laugh about it. I trembled for hours, as I'm sure Shari, Jonathan's fiancée, did when she saw the story on *Good Morning America* the next day.

Behind the Scenes

While the violent attacks and death threats escalated, so did the hecklers who threw pies in his face. When he couldn't duck fast enough, Jerry stopped, tasted the pie, made a joke, and continued speaking.

While the vast majority of the criticisms seemed targeted toward God, Jerry took plenty of hits from fellow Christians, as well. One fellow minister called him the most dangerous man in America, and the Fundamental Baptist Fellowship International wrote a resolution that said in part, "Moral reformation is not the mission of the Church, but instead the preaching of the saving grace of Christ." Yet, no matter what people said or did, Jerry never held grudges and always greeted these people with kindness and warmth.

What some in America thought was that Jerry was a stern, hate-filled extremist who opposed everything and everyone. Americans also saw Jerry being interviewed numerous times on *Larry King Live, The Phil Donahue Show,* and every other major talk show in the nation. Viewers must have tuned in to those broadcasts and thought the hosts despised Jerry, but that wasn't the case. Duke Westover traveled with Jerry to most of those interviews and witnessed the real story as it unfolded behind the scenes.

"Jerry's relationship with Phil Donahue was representative of most of the people who interviewed him," Duke explains. "Talk show hosts knew that Jerry was a controversial figure, and controversy made good television. That's why Phil had Jerry on his show numerous times. One Monday morning I got a call from Phil's producer, Gail. She said that their guest for Wednesday's show had canceled at the last minute and she wanted me to ask if Jerry would fill the slot.

"Jerry tried, whenever possible, to accept national interviews because he believed in taking every opportunity to preach the gospel to millions of people on someone else's nickel. The person interviewing him might show Jerry in the worst possible light, but if Jerry could work the gospel message into the conversation, he didn't care. So I wasn't surprised when Jerry agreed to go on Phil's show at the last minute.

"When we arrived, Phil said, 'Jerry, I've got nothing—no show. Have you said anything controversial lately?'

" 'Well, yes,' Jerry said, explaining the latest thing that had his critics in an uproar.

" 'That's good,' Phil said, 'what can we do with it?'

"Jerry thought for a few moments and said, 'I'll take this position, and you take the opposite one.' Jerry outlined the show before they went on the air. With the cameras rolling, they did the show as Jerry suggested and anyone would have assumed that Phil despised Jerry. When they finished filming, Phil walked over to Jerry and gave him a hug. 'You saved me, Jerry. I don't know how to thank you.' "

This kind of thing happened time and time again. The host would spend the entire show attacking and arguing with Jerry, but once the cameras were off the same man would talk to Jerry about personal problems and ask for his counsel. That was true of even political enemies. Men like Jesse Jackson and Al Sharpton counted themselves among Jerry's friends . . . behind the scenes.

A Fool for the Gospel

Most people who met Jerry ended up liking and respecting him, but that wasn't always the case. Bill Maher was a whole different breed of talk show host. Jonathan, who traveled with Jerry a great deal, remembers having a hard time watching the way Bill Maher treated his father.

"I flew to California with Dad to be on the *Politically Incorrect* show with Bill Maher," Jonathan remembers. "I'd seen Dad interviewed a lot, but had never witnessed anything like the way he was treated both on and off the air of this show. Bill Maher was rude and disrespectful and did everything in his power to try to fit Dad into the caricature that the media had painted of him.

"When we left the studio I was upset. 'Dad, why do you put yourself through that?' I asked. 'It was awful and demeaning.'

" 'Jonathan,' Dad said, 'what you say is true. But I just preached the gospel to millions of people tonight, and Bill Maher paid for it.' "

Jerry was willing to be made a fool for the sake of the gospel.

Building Bridges

Another interesting relationship existed between Jerry and Dr. Mel White. Mel was a well-known author and ghostwriter who had written for Jerry in the past, as well as for Billy Graham, D. James Kennedy, Oliver North, and Pat Robertson.

Later, Mel and his wife divorced and he came out of the closet as a homosexual. He started Soulforce, an organization designed to confront intolerance toward the gay community. Although Jerry and Mel had a good relationship, Mel wanted Jerry to stop preaching that homosexuality was a sin. That was never going to happen.

What both men did agree on, however, was that there was too much violence on both sides of the issue. They each wanted to see more tolerance and peace between the factions. In 1999 Mel asked Jerry for a meeting. He added that if Jerry refused to meet with him, he and his supporters would picket Thomas Road and Liberty University, protesting in the streets and labeling Jerry as someone not willing to dialogue with pro-homosexual forces. Mel wrote a letter to Dr. Ron Godwin saying that he was coming—one way or the other. To dialogue or to protest.

Threats of protest held no sway over Jerry. We'd been picketed so many times that it simply made no difference. Jerry knew Mel well enough to know that nothing he could say would change Mel's mind. Likewise, because the Bible calls homosexuality a sin, Jerry would never change his stance. However, he believed in building bridges, so he agreed to the meeting.

On October 21, 1999, Dr. Mel White and his companion Gary Nixon arrived at Jerry's office. Among those present was Dr. Godwin, who recounts the event.

"We sat on the porch and talked," Dr Godwin recalls. "Doc was warm and friendly, and listened to everything Mel had to say, letting him state his full case. Mel said that homosexuals deserved tolerance and acceptance, and that they were Christians with a different interpretation of the Bible.

"When Mel finished speaking, Jerry acknowledged that everyone deserved tolerance, and he restated his position: 'Homosexuality is a sin,' he said, 'but no more a sin than adultery.' However, he said, the Bible defines marriage as existing between one man and one woman.

" 'If one of my children came and said that they were gay,' Jerry explained, 'I would love them. I would never turn my back on them. My door would always be open to them. But I would tell them that their lifestyle was a sin. And I would pray for them.' "

Jerry loved Mel as a friend, but could not condone his lifestyle. The conversation was kind and polite, but in the end both men agreed to disagree.

In a demonstration of tolerance, Jerry invited Mel and a large group of his supporters from the gay and lesbian community to a reception with members of Thomas Road Baptist Church. The forum took place just two days later, on October 23, 1999, in the church's gymnasium. Several hundred members of Thomas Road greeted two hundred gays, lesbians, and transvestites. Over refreshments, the two groups mingled and got acquainted. A good number of our church members invited the visitors to stay in their homes.

The gathering was nonconfrontational as the two groups enjoyed getting to know one another. Mel got a lot of national media at-

> *I looked across the room and saw Dr. and Mrs. Falwell having a warm, animated conversation with a 6' 7" transvestite. They were as comfortable and friendly with him as with anyone they'd ever met. They only differed in their definition of sin.*
>
> —DR. RON GODWIN

tention and support for the gay coalition from the event. As time passed, Mel pressed Jerry for more meetings. Because Jerry didn't believe that either side was going to change its stance, and because he felt that Mel was just trying to generate media attention to gain support for his cause, he refused to grant any other meetings.

Mel later moved to Lynchburg and bought a house across the street from Thomas Road Baptist Church. On Sunday mornings people with placards portraying gay slogans paced in his lawn. Mel attended church with us for years. He was quiet and respectful during services. But whenever Jerry preached against the sin of homosexuality, Mel stood in silent protest. In time, he stopped attending the services.

When Jerry died, Mel wrote, "I was in the dentist's chair when I heard that Jerry Falwell passed away. I couldn't believe that I started crying. I had to find an office and I just cried."

The Preacher and the Pornographer

Without a doubt, the most high-profile enemy Jerry ever won as a friend was Larry Flynt, the publisher of *Hustler* magazine.

You might wonder what a conservative, fundamentalist preacher could possibly have in common with one of America's leading porn dealers. The answer is, more than you'd think. Jerry was born and raised in Virginia, Larry in Kentucky. Jerry's father sold bootleg liquor, as did Larry at one time. Both men were the sons of alcoholic fathers. From those similar beginnings their lives had taken opposite roads, but Jerry understood that without his mother's prayers that might not have been the case.

The legal battle between Larry and Jerry would never have happened had Larry never run in *Hustler* the parody intimating that Jerry's first sexual encounter had been with his mother. Jerry had no trouble shrugging off the insults and innuendos that came his way, but you do not drag the name of a southern gentleman's mother through the mud without a fight. Jerry sued for libel and won the case. Larry took the case to a federal appeals court, where Jerry won again. Larry appealed a second time and lost. The case traveled all the way to the Supreme Court, which ruled unanimously in favor of *Hustler.* They said that Jerry was a public figure, which made him (and his mother) fair game.

The long legal battle not only made headline news, it ended up on the big screen. Hollywood put it to film in *The People vs. Larry Flynt* (1996). But where the movie ended wasn't where the story ended. Later, Jerry and Larry traveled around the country debating the issues in public forums. Jonathan attended many of the debates. One debate at the National Newspaper Association in Boca Raton, Florida, stands out in his mind.

"After the debate," Jonathan recalls, "Larry Flynt offered to fly us home on his big, black Gulfstream IV jet, and we took him up on his offer. I watched Dad and Larry sit across from one another and talk during that whole flight, and it wasn't a debate. Here were two men who fought one another all the way to the Supreme Court, but now they were discussing football and politics.

"On another occasion I'd flown to California with Dad, and while we were there he called Larry. 'Hey, I'm in town and thought I'd come by if you're free.' Before long I found myself walking into Larry's massive office, which had a huge desk, Oriental rugs, a chandelier, and some of the most incredible sculptures I'd ever seen. Across Larry's desk were all the latest issues of his porno-

MY ENEMIES, MY FRIENDS

graphic magazines. Dad hated pornography, but he liked Larry Flynt, the king of porn. I thought theirs was the most interesting relationship I'd ever seen. They sat and talked for a couple of hours that day. At one point, Larry suggested that Dad try a diet that had helped him, and he had his secretary download it for him.

"On our flight home, I asked Dad why he worked at keeping a relationship with Larry. Dad looked at me, a thoughtful expression on his face, and said, 'One day Larry Flynt will come to a place in his life when he needs a friend. And there will come a time when he needs something of a spiritual nature. When that happens, I want to be the man he calls.' "

Years later, after Jerry had died, we received an outpouring of calls from many well-known people, such as George and Barbara Bush, President George W. Bush, Ted Kennedy, Jesse Jackson, and many other people with whom Jerry had formed a friendship over the years. But another response that meant a great deal to our family was what Larry Flynt wrote in the *Los Angeles Times*—not because it painted Jerry in a good light, because it did not. We appreciated it, though, because in the end Larry called Jerry his friend, and nothing would have pleased Jerry more.

Here is the complete article.

LARRY FLYNT: MY FRIEND, JERRY FALWELL

By Larry Flynt, LARRY FLYNT is the publisher of Hustler *magazine and the author of "Sex, Lies and Politics." May 20, 2007*

The first time the Rev. Jerry Falwell put his hands on me, I was stunned. Not only had we been archenemies for fifteen years, his beliefs and mine traveling in different solar systems, and not only had he sued me for $50 million (a case I lost repeatedly yet eventually won in the Supreme Court), but now he was hugging me in front of millions on the Larry King show.

It was 1997. My autobiography, "An Unseemly Man," had just been published, describing my life as a publisher of pornography. The film "The People vs. Larry Flynt" had recently come out, and the country was well aware of the battle that Falwell and I had fought: a battle that had changed the laws governing what the American public can see and hear in the media and that had dramatically strengthened our right to free speech.

King was conducting the interview. It was the first time since the infamous 1988 trial that the reverend and I had been in the same room together, and the thought of even breathing the same air with him made me sick. I disagreed with Falwell (who died last week) on absolutely everything he preached, and he looked at me as symbolic of all the social ills that a society can possibly have. But I'd do anything to sell the book and the film, and Falwell would do anything to preach, so King's audience of 8 million viewers was all the incentive either of us needed to bring us together.

But let's start at the beginning and flash back to the late 1970s, when the battle between Falwell, the leader of the Moral Majority, and I first began. I was publishing Hustler magazine, which most people know has been pushing the envelope of taste from the very beginning, and Falwell was blasting me every chance he had. He would talk about how I was a slime dealer responsible for the decay of all morals. He called me every terrible name he could think of—names as bad, in my opinion, as any language used in my magazine.

After several years of listening to him bash me and reading his insults, I decided it was time to start poking some fun at him. So we ran a parody ad in Hustler—a takeoff on the then-current Campari ads in which people were interviewed describing "their first time." In the ads, it ultimately became clear that the interviewees were describing their first time sipping Campari. But not in our parody. We had Falwell describing his "first time" as having been with his mother, "drunk off our God-fearing [expletive deleted]" in an outhouse.

Apparently, the reverend didn't find the joke funny. He sued us for libel in federal court in Virginia, claiming that the magazine had inflicted emotional stress on him. It was a long and tedious fight, beginning in 1983 and ending in 1988, but Hustler Magazine Inc. vs. Jerry Falwell was without question my most important battle.

We lost in our initial jury trial, and we lost again in federal appeals court. After spending a fortune, everyone's advice to me was to just settle the case and be done, but I wasn't listening; I wasn't about to pay Falwell $200,000 for hurting his feelings or, as his lawyers called it, "intentional infliction of emotional distress." We appealed to the U.S. 4th Circuit Court of Appeals, and I lost for a third time.

Everyone was certain this was the end. We never thought the U.S. Supreme Court would agree to hear the case. But it did, and though I felt doomed throughout the trial and was convinced that I was going to lose, we never gave up. As we had moved up the judicial ladder, this case had become much more than just a personal battle between a pornographer and a preacher, because the first Amendment was so much at the heart of the case.

To my amazement, we won. It wasn't until after I won the case and read the justices' unanimous decision in my favor that I realized fully the significance of what had happened. The justices held that a parody of a public figure was protected under the first Amendment even if it was outrageous, even if it was "doubtless gross and repugnant," as they put it, and even if it was designed to inflict emotional distress. In a unanimous decision— written by, of all people, Chief Justice William H. Rehnquist—the court reasoned that if it supported Falwell's lower-court victory, no one would ever have to prove something was false and libelous to win a judgment. All anyone would have to prove is that "he upset me" or "she made me feel bad." The lawsuits would be endless, and that would be the end of free speech.

Everyone was shocked at our victory—and no one more so than Falwell, who on the day of the decision called me a "sleaze merchant" hiding behind the first Amendment. Still, over time, Falwell was forced to publicly come to grips with the reality that this is America, where you can make fun of anyone you want. That hadn't been absolutely clear before our case, but now it's being taught in law schools all over the country, and our case is being hailed as one of the most important free-speech cases of the twentieth century.

No wonder that when he started hugging me and smooching me on television ten years later, I was a bit confused. I hadn't seen him since we'd been in court together, and that night I didn't see him until I came out on the stage. I was expecting (and looking for) a fight, but instead he was putting his hands all over me. I remember thinking, "I spent $3 million taking that case to the Supreme Court, and now this guy wants to put his hand on my leg?"

Soon after that episode, I was in my office in Beverly Hills, and out of nowhere my secretary buzzes me, saying, "Jerry Falwell is here to see you." I was shocked, but I said, "Send him in." We talked for two hours, with the latest issues of

Hustler neatly stacked on my desk in front of him. He suggested that we go around the country debating, and I agreed. We went to colleges, debating moral issues and first Amendment issues—what's "proper," what's not and why.

In the years that followed and up until his death, he'd come to see me every time he was in California. We'd have interesting philosophical conversations. We'd exchange personal Christmas cards. He'd show me pictures of his grandchildren. I was with him in Florida once when he complained about his health and his weight, so I suggested that he go on a diet that had worked for me. I faxed a copy to his wife when I got back home.

The truth is, the reverend and I had a lot in common. He was from Virginia, and I was from Kentucky. His father had been a bootlegger, and I had been one too in my twenties before I went into the Navy. We steered our conversations away from politics, but religion was within bounds. He wanted to save me and was determined to get me out of "the business."

My mother always told me that no matter how repugnant you find a person, when you meet them face to face you will always find something about them to like. The more I got to know Falwell, the more I began to see that his public portrayals were caricatures of himself. There was a dichotomy between the real Falwell and the one he showed the public.

He was definitely selling brimstone religion and would do anything to add another member to his mailing list. But in the end, I knew what he was selling, and he knew what I was selling, and we found a way to communicate.

I always kicked his [expletive deleted] about his crazy ideas and the things he said. Every time I'd call him, I'd get put right through, and he'd let me berate him about his views. When he was getting blasted for his ridiculous homophobic comments after he wrote his "Tinky Winky" article cautioning parents that the purple Teletubby character was in fact gay, I called him in Florida and yelled at him to "leave the Tinky Winkies alone."

When he referred to Ellen Degeneres in print as Ellen "Degenerate," I called him and said, "What are you doing? You don't need to poison the whole lake with your venom." I could hear him mumbling out of the side of his mouth, "These lesbians just drive me crazy." I'm sure I never changed his mind about anything, just as he never changed mine.

I'll never admire him for his views or his opinions. To this day, I'm not sure if his television embrace was meant to mend fences, to show himself to the public as a generous and forgiving preacher or merely to make me uneasy, but the ultimate result was one I never expected and was just as shocking a turn to me as was winning that famous Supreme Court case: We became friends.

CHAPTER EIGHT

Surviving the PTL Scandal

Reporters from all over the globe flooded Lynchburg on March 20, 1987. Camera crews sent live feed via satellite to television networks and cable news services. Every phone line at Thomas Road Baptist Church was lit up with calls from newspaper, radio, and television networks. Reporters carrying video cameras and tape recorders dogged Jerry's steps, on the scent of a story—and it was a big one.

After eight years in the political spotlight, Jerry's work with the Moral Majority was winding down. With a deep sigh of relief, he had looked forward to focusing his attention on Thomas Road Baptist Church and Liberty University. None of us imagined that his respite would be so brief.

Black clouds gathered on the horizon before we knew much more than the names of Jim and Tammy Faye Bakker. Except for the fact that both Jim and Jerry were preachers with a presence on Christian television, the two men had little in common. Jerry was a fundamental Baptist, and Jim was a charismatic and member of the Assemblies of God.

Once on a family vacation we'd driven through Heritage Village without stopping, which sums up our contact with that ministry. Jerry and Jim had spoken only a few words in passing over the years when they'd attended meetings of the National Religious Broadcasters. They didn't know each other and were not friends.

Jerry's years in the media spotlight made him concerned about the rumors that were flying about Jim Bakker and PTL. The PTL (short for "Praise the Lord") Club was the television ministry run by Jim and Tammy Faye Bakker. He understood the damage that lies, innuendos, and distorted truths could do any ministry. He'd heard that over the years the *Charlotte Observer* had been unfair to the Bakkers. Jerry assumed that this was another example of irresponsible journalism smearing Christian conservatives. Even if the accusations weren't true, they had the power to hurt not only Jim Bakker but all televangelists, and Christianity as well.

The Calm Before the Storm

Although Jerry was concerned about the situation, the cloud hanging over PTL had not yet cast its shadow over Lynchburg or any of our ministries. Then Jerry got word from Warren Marcus, who ran our television ministry. Warren said that Jim Bakker's right-hand man, Richard Dortch, wanted to meet with him. Jerry's schedule was packed and he couldn't make the meeting, so he sent several men from his staff to represent him. One of them was Mark DeMoss, Jerry's executive assistant at the time.

"Before the PTL scandal," Mark recalls, "a church in Bangor, Maine, had asked for Jerry's help when its pastor suffered a moral failure. Jerry had temporarily stepped into leadership at the church in Maine, traveling there to preach and counsel the pastor. He'd done a good job, and news of how he'd helped that ministry reached Richard Dortch at PTL. I was one of the men Jerry sent to meet with him that day. Dortch said that the *Charlotte Observer* was about to release a terrible story about Jim Bakker having an affair with a church secretary."

The Bible has specific instructions for handling accusations against a fellow Christian. If a brother sins against another Christian, the two of them are to discuss it first alone. If the one in the wrong doesn't repent, two or three Christian brothers are to go speak to him. As far as Jerry could determine, no Christian brothers had gone to Jim in private to discuss the allegations raised by the article.

In March 1987, Jerry and several other men flew out to meet with Jim and Tammy Bakker. Jerry met with Jim alone first, and asked him about the accusations. Jim told Jerry that seven years earlier he'd had a brief encounter with Jessica Hahn in a hotel room, but that no sexual act had been consummated. He acted repentant, and told Jerry that he had repented to God and to Tammy and that both of them had forgiven him. He assured Jerry that no hush money had been paid to anyone, and that no one had been raped.

A few moments later, when the two men rejoined the rest of

the group, Jim Bakker made a surprise announcement: "Jerry, I want you to take over PTL. I'm going to step down, and I'll place my ministry in your hands tomorrow." He went on to ask that Richard Dortch and Rex Humbard be appointed to the new board, and that Jerry appoint the remaining members.

Everyone on both sides was stunned. Jerry finally agreed to step in—because he thought Jim's absence would be temporary and he wanted to minimize the damage to Christian ministries.

In order to get an interview with Jim Bakker, the *Charlotte Observer* agreed to hold their story for a week. Jerry flew home from his meeting with the Bakkers and we talked and prayed through most of the night.

The next morning, Jack Wyrtzen, who'd founded Word of Life Fellowship in Schroon Lake, New York, spoke at Liberty's chapel service. Afterward, Jerry described to Jack the situation with PTL.

"It looks like the Lord has opened this door, Jerry," Jack said, "and you're the only man I know who would dare walk through it." Jerry continued his own television program, *Old Time Gospel Hour*, while stepping into the chair at PTL.

Jerry's new PTL board included Rex Humbard and Richard Dortch, as Jim Bakker had requested. In addition, Jerry appointed to the board James Watt, former secretary of the interior; Sam Moore, then president of Thomas Nelson publishing; Ben Armstrong, executive director of the National Religious Broadcasters; Charles Stanley, former president of the Southern Baptist Convention; Jerry Lipps, owner of Lipps Trucking; Thomas Zimmerman, a leader in the Assemblies of God; Richard Lee, pastor of Rehoboth Baptist Church in Atlanta; DeWitt Braud, a board member of *Old Time Gospel Hour*; and one of Jerry's associates, Jerry Nims.

The next day Jerry told our children and key people in our lives about his involvement with PTL. He sensed that this would be a mess of mammoth proportions, but felt that Jim's seeming humble and repentant was an important first step in the process, and he felt he should step in to help.

Jerry's first clue that Jim Bakker had lied to him occurred when Jim's confession was printed in the *Charlotte Observer.* Jim's tone was belligerent rather than repentant. Instead of confessing his sins, he blamed everyone else for his problems. He also resigned from the Assemblies of God. Jerry believed this was because they were investigating the charges and were about to find more unpleasant surprises.

Jim said in print, "I sorrowfully acknowledge that seven years ago, in an isolated incident, I was wickedly manipulated by treacherous former friends and colleagues who victimized me with the aid of a female confederate. They conspired to betray me into a sexual encounter. . . . In retrospect, it was poor judgment to have succumbed to blackmail."

Later in the interview he admitted to paying money to "protect and spare the ministry and my family, and to avoid further suffering or hurt anyone to appease these persons who were determined to destroy this ministry."

Jerry laid down the newspa-

> *I had just made the most difficult and controversial decision of my lifetime in ministry. Neither my friends nor my enemies would understand. Once again I would find myself in the middle of a media firestorm. By involving myself in the PTL scandal, I was risking our ministry in Lynchburg. We had no idea what price we would pay.*
>
> —JERRY FALWELL

per, closed his eyes, and pressed his fingers against the bridge of his nose. Everything Jim Bakker told him had been a lie.

New Accusations

By March 20, reporters from around the world had set up camp in Lynchburg for Jerry's press conference. He had promised them a full accounting of the situation. He sent auditors to investigate PTL records, but the auditors were stonewalled. Even though Jerry was chairman of the board, most of the information he requested never arrived.

Disgruntled PTL employees called our home at all hours of the night. Among other things, they reported that they'd been instructed not to cooperate with Jerry or any of his representatives. They said that all sensitive materials were being shredded. Jerry hadn't known the Bakker's close friends and associates, but when he met with them he saw that their grief and pain were real. He sympathized with them as more stories about sexual and financial misconduct surfaced.

> *I knew a terrible storm was brewing, and I hated to think that once again I would be God's lightning rod at the center of that storm.*
>
> —JERRY FALWELL

Donations to *Old Time Gospel Hour* dropped by more than $2 million, and the credibility of all media ministries had fallen. Jerry was ready to throw in the towel and resign—when he learned that Jim was about to reinstate himself as chairman and return as host of PTL.

On April 23, Jerry, Mark DeMoss, and Jerry Nims flew to

Nashville for a meeting with Reverend John Ankerberg. A group of people had gathered there to discuss charges to which they were ready to testify. In that meeting, the board learned that the Jessica Hahn incident seven years earlier had been only the tip of the sexual scandal iceberg. The specific charges left Jerry speechless.

The next evening, Jerry and I were sitting at Liberty's junior-senior banquet, when Mark DeMoss called him out of the room. "Reverend Ankerberg is on the *Larry King Live* show," Mark said, "and he's sharing all the charges that were made in Nashville."

Already, rumors had been circulating that Jerry was trying to take over PTL, which was not true. Jerry had one mega-ministry and didn't want another, especially one shrouded in scandal. Now, with Ankerberg on the air detailing the charges, both men were seen as conspiring to hurt Jim Bakker.

> *What I had learned made me physically ill. The PTL tragedy had the possibility of becoming the worst public scandal in Christian history.*
>
> —JERRY FALWELL

When journalists asked Reverend Ankerberg if Jerry had known what he was going to say on *Larry King,* he replied, "How could Falwell know when I didn't know myself? Larry King only invited me to be on the show a few hours before we were on the air."

However, most of the media ignored the facts. On April 23, Jim Bakker demanded that Jerry turn over PTL. He wrote in part, "I will not fight you if you ignore my wishes, but I must let you know that what you are embarking on will truly start what the press has labeled a 'holy war.' "

Jerry had done only what the PTL board had appointed him to do. But it seemed as though Jim Bakker had pressed the destruct button and was methodically destroying his own life and ministry. By the end of April, Jerry seldom slept at all. He asked me if I thought he should resign from PTL, but I didn't pretend to know God's will in the situation.

Jonathan, on the other hand, said, "Don't you dare quit!"

Other friends cried, "Get out!"

Reverend Bailey Smith, former president of the Southern Baptist Convention, said in an interview: "It comes to a point where it really doesn't matter whether some things are true. If the perception is true, it hurts his integrity. Bakker, I think, has lost the right to lead. He needs to be forgiven, but the place of leadership is another matter."

A Hard and Narrow Road

The last Saturday in April, Jerry slept only two hours. He knew that if he was going to resign, he had to do it at the upcoming board meeting. If he didn't resign then, he would have to ride out the storm. That night I held Jerry's hand and we watched the sun come up. Jerry later admitted that it had been the longest night of his life, but he still didn't know if he should resign.

When he asked me my opinion, I stated the obvious. "Who else could do the job?"

Jerry flew to Charlotte for the board meeting still unsure of what God wanted him to do. But that morning a verse kept rolling over and over in his mind. "But Jesus said to him, 'No one, having put his hand to the plow, and looking back, is fit for the kingdom of God' " (Luke 9:62). By the time the meeting was called to order, Jerry knew God wanted him to stay on as chairman of PTL.

That meeting was most revealing. Among other things, Jerry learned that Reverend Richard Dortch—Jim Bakker's successor, the show's host, and PTL president—had approved a scheme to pay Jessica Hahn $265,000 to buy her silence. Dortch had conspired with Roe Messner to hide the money in a building invoice. Messner, who later become Tammy's second husband, would ultimately go to prison for bankruptcy fraud.

At the end of the meeting, Jerry terminated Jim and Tammy Bakker's contract with PTL.

"The decision to sever the Bakkers from PTL was very difficult," Mark DeMoss explains. "Although Jerry didn't condone the sin, he respected the personal sacrifice Jim and Tammy had made while pioneering Christian television, hosting the PTL Club, and building Heritage USA. In addition, Jerry believed that the Bakkers had a great concept. He could imagine Heritage Village attracting top Christian speakers and musicians. Although he didn't

---

As the evidence piled up, I knew for certain that there was no easy way to escape the consequences of the financial mismanagement and sexual misconduct that plagued the ministry. No aspirin could end the pain. No simple bandage could bind the wounds. Radical surgery was required to save PTL, and as the meeting progressed it became more evident that the radical surgery would have to begin with the Bakkers themselves.

—JERRY FALWELL

see any way to restore Jim and Tammy, he hoped to find a way to salvage their dream.

"I was a twenty-five-year-old kid in the center of this thing, flying back and forth between Lynchburg and Charlotte in a whirlwind from early morning until late at night. I was physically and mentally exhausted, yet Jerry was fifty-four years old and was still fulfilling his duties as pastor of Thomas Road Baptist Church and as chancellor of Liberty University. I don't see how he did it."

In addition to multiplying charges of sexual misconduct, there were pending investigations by the U.S. Attorney's office, the FBI, and the Internal Revenue Service. By then they'd found $70 million in debts facing the toppling ministry. The new board's audits revealed a hidden executive payroll account that had released large sums of money to Jim and Tammy over the years. Jerry and the new board of PTL were named in a class action lawsuit for $601 million. They, it seemed, were guilty by association.

As every accusation began to be borne out in fact, Jerry came to realize that the *Charlotte Observer* had been fair and honest in all their reporting, and he respected how they handled the situation.

On Tuesday, May 26, Jim and Tammy Bakker appeared with Ted Koppel on *Nightline,* and charged Jerry with stealing their ministry. Jim downplayed his sexual encounter with Jessica Hahn. When Koppel asked them about alleged bonuses of $1.9 million paid to the couple in 1986, Bakker retorted, "Jim and Tammy are a tad flamboyant."

When Jerry fired them, the Bakkers requested severance pay of $300,000 a

> *I felt like a juggler keeping eight balls in the air simultaneously and wondering when one or all of them would fall on my own head.*
>
> —JERRY FALWELL

year for life for Jim, and $100,000 for Tammy. They requested life insurance, health insurance, bodyguards, rights to any books, their house and furniture, secretarial help, and maid service.

There was no evidence of repentance.

The Dam Was Breaking

While Jerry once had sympathy for the Bakkers, he was now concerned that they would once again gain financial control of the ministry. He felt that PTL partners had been victimized enough. So, with the ministry on the verge of financial disaster, Jerry opposed bankruptcy—until he realized that there was no way for the ministry to survive without protection of its assets. Bankruptcy would give PTL a chance to reorganize without creditors forcing them to sell off the assets piece by piece.

Meanwhile, Jim and Tammy hired a criminal lawyer, Melvin Belli, to represent them in regaining control of PTL. In a televised confrontation with PTL attorney Norman Roy Grutman, Mr. Belli heard the real case against the Bakkers and walked off the set. He ceased to be their lawyer. The Bakkers went into seclusion while criminal charges were filed. Jim Bakker and other Christian leaders went to jail, and Christianity suffered a black eye.

During that summer and fall, the new board raised millions of dollars to try to prop up PTL, but it wasn't enough to plug the hole in the financial dyke. In October, having done all they could to save the ministry, Jerry and the entire board resigned.

Over the next few years Jerry spent a lot of time soul-searching about whether he'd misunderstood God's will by stepping in to help PTL. The scandal had put Liberty at risk financially. Indeed, the whole incident had had a negative effect on giving to most ministries in America, whether they were on TV or not.

Jerry's reason for stepping into the PTL scandal had been to save the ministry and minimize the damage to the gospel of Christ. But after it all played out, Jerry began to feel that God hadn't sent him to save PTL but to put a stop to the immorality and financial fraud. Without the kind of strong leadership Jerry had provided, the sin and corruption would have continued. And without accountability, an unrepentant Jim Bakker might have regained control of the ministry and the money.

Much later, Jerry visited Jim in prison. This time, he was convinced that Bakker's repentance was genuine.

Free Fall

Following his resignation from the board of PTL, Jerry returned home exhausted. He looked at me and said, "I need my family." After listening to the way those men had used Jessica Hahn and the way thousands of Christians had been bilked out of their money, Jerry—like King David in the Bible—asked God to restore his soul. He settled into his home and office like a man on death row who'd just been given a reprieve.

On one of our family vacations to Myrtle Beach, Jonathan wanted to go bungee jumping. We scoped out several places before choosing the right one. I watched Jonathan climb a scaffold high into the sky and felt my heart stutter as he dove off the platform, only to be caught by the bungee cord before he hit bottom. Jeannie stood on the platform and weighed the risks. "If you jump, I'll jump!" Jerry shouted from below.

Jeannie sailed off that platform as though she were jumping into her father's arms.

Jerry, dressed in his usual suit and tie, climbed the scaffold. Instead of facing the front as everyone else had done, Jerry backed up to the edge of the platform the way you might see a diver do at the Olympics, standing on the balls of his feet and ready to thrust himself into the air. Without pausing to give it thought, Jerry's face lit with laughter as he fell backward with his arms splayed out on both sides—a free fall, back first, face upward, smiling toward God.

That's how he lives his life, I thought. *His life is a free fall into his Father's arms. He has absolute faith that God will catch him.*

After Jerry climbed down, the family turned to leave. Suddenly I heard myself say in a small voice, "What about me?" They all turned back with puzzled looks. *You want to bungee jump?*

I understood the question mark on each of their faces, because the older I'd gotten the fewer risks I'd been willing to take. I was not the risk taker. I was the one who wrung her hands in the background. But something had stirred in me watching Jerry fall backward into the air. Perhaps it was the symbolism that prompted me to grab the ladder with white-knuckle fists and, refusing to look down, climb up and up and up, until I found myself trembling on the platform high above them.

I remember the smell of the sea and the feel of the heavy bungee cord. The warm sun shone on me but did nothing to warm the chill that threatened to turn me to ice from the inside out. I did not take a running powerful jump like Jonathan. I did not make a graceful swan dive like Jeannie. I did not free-fall backward like Jerry. As much as I wished to be like them, I was . . . me. I squeezed my eyes tight, wrapped my arms around myself, and stepped off into thin air.

I fell . . . fell, and fell some more before the bungee cord yanked me like a rag doll and jerked me high into the air, each bounce ending with the stomach-in-your-throat feeling you get when an elevator falls in rapid descent.

That's how I live my life, I thought as my feet touched the ground and my family rushed to me, delighted with my courage. *I follow in Jerry's wake, eyes squeezed tight, and step off into what feels like thin air knowing that in the end I can trust him . . . always.*

Jerry wrapped his arms around me, threw his head back, and laughed with delight. Jerry always said that I was his rudder and his brakes, but he's the one who gave me the courage to soar.

Return to Normal

As Jerry settled into life after PTL, I tried to wrap him in just what he needed . . . normalcy. Although Jerry had friends all the way up in the White House, at home he had friends no less dear. These friends surrounded him with a faithfulness that was like a balm to his wounded soul.

One such man was Leo Cawthorne. Leo was a quiet man who worked behind the scenes. In 1968, he'd helped repair the church buses that collected

Jerry always said that I was his rudder and his brakes, but he's the one who gave me the courage to soar.

—MACEL FALWELL

children for Sunday school. The following year he'd run the camera for the interpreter of the deaf. He also sold tickets for our Living Christmas Tree program.

Once, years ago, Jerry walked into church with dirty shoes. Leo rushed out and bought shoe polish and went to work polishing them. Every Sunday for the next twenty years, Leo polished Jerry's shoes, and always refused payment for his services. Jerry made up a business card for him that read, "Leo Cawthorne, Assistant to Jerry Falwell."

After PTL, the *swish-swish* of Leo's brush on Jerry's shoes each Sunday morning was just the kind of normalcy Jerry needed, and Leo's quiet demeanor was filled with peace.

Of course, the annual pig pickin' was another dose of normal for Jerry. That historic gathering came about after I heard the term *pig pickin'* somewhere and wondered what it meant. I figured if anyone knew what a pig pickin' was it would be my friend Dot Davis.

"Of course I know what a pig pickin' is!" Dot said when I asked her about it.

"I figured you would."

"What's *that* supposed to mean?"

I chuckled. "Well, what is it then?"

"It's a custom from the Deep South," Dot explained. "It's like a big barbecue. You roast a whole hog, make lots of side dishes, and invite everyone you know."

> When my husband, Leo, was a teenager, Jerry was youth pastor at Park Avenue Baptist Church, and he used to pick Leo up from his home at 1113 Pierce Street. Fifteen years later, we joined Thomas Road Baptist Church. Jerry took one look at Leo and said, "1113 Pierce Street!"
>
> —PATSY CAWTHORNE

"Oh . . . ," I said, weak with gratitude that I'd never had to resort to a pig pickin' for food.

That evening, Dot hatched a plan with her husband, Gene. "Let's have a pig pickin'," she suggested, and they started planning the event. Every fall for the next eighteen years, we got an invitation to an honest to goodness pig pickin'.

Jerry loved the southern cooking on tables laden with food and the good-hearted ribbing I took every year because it had been my question that had prompted the event. After his tour of duty on behalf of PTL, I watched Jerry relax at the normalcy of our next pig pickin'. There, among friends, he didn't have to deal with reporters following him or worry that something he said might end up on the next day's news.

The Ladies

Another part of normalcy was Jerry's ongoing amusement over the antics of the ladies in my close circle of friends. Watching color come back into his face made all of us only too happy to make him laugh.

Our group, formed in 1978, included Dot Davis, Lurline Braud, Beverly Lowry, Sue Evans, Patsy Cawthorne, Shirley Burton, and my sister-in-law, Carol Pate. We started out meeting for lunch on each of our

> *Jerry and Macel have always been there for us. They stood by me when my mother died, when my brother died, and when my husband died suddenly sixteen months ago. I haven't held a pig pickin' since.*
>
> —DOT DAVIS

birthdays, which is a custom we still keep. We agreed to throw one another baby showers, and one for the first child born to each of our children, which means that by now we are the first ladies of baby showers and should write a book on the subject.

One year I was elected district president of the Virginia Federation of Women's Clubs. Of course I roped this group of women into helping me. They also helped me raise money for our Christian Academy.

Each year Jerry held a Super Conference for pastors and church leaders across the nation. For the conference we served breakfast, lunch, and dinner. The ladies didn't let me cook, but I helped organize the event and handled the money. The ladies made soup and chili in five-gallon containers. They stirred up an amazing array of baked goods, and even wrote a cookbook.

Before Easter we made and sold beautiful monogrammed Easter eggs. We also wrapped and sold Thanksgiving and Christmas baskets. With our earnings, we bought the school an air conditioner, finished a room for the teachers, bought playground equipment, and held Teacher's Appreciation Day.

I know that sounds like a lot of work, and it was, but you would

> *I didn't know Macel when my oldest daughter, Karen, had to have heart surgery when she was six years old. We took her to Baltimore for surgery, and she came out severely brain damaged. Jerry phoned us every single night that we spent in Baltimore. When we got Karen home, she required a type of physical therapy called patterning, and we needed volunteers to help. Every week, Macel came and worked with Karen.*
>
> —PATSY CAWTHORNE

> *When my daughter lost her baby, Jerry and Macel were there with her.*
> —BEVERLY LOWRY

have to know my friends to understand how they could turn the most tedious task into a fest of sidesplitting laughter.

In addition to our fund-raising efforts, we formed a group exercise class and hired a female trainer to work with us. We had to discontinue that after a while, though. I'm not saying she gave up on us . . . Let's just say we turned our attention to other things, things that didn't hurt or make us sweat.

In 1983, Jerry and I had been invited to the National Religious Broadcasters (NRB) convention in Washington, D.C. "Jerry," I said when we got the invitation, "let's take the ladies!"

"Okay," Jerry replied, grinning at the prospect.

I announced to the group that we were all going to Washington, D.C., but I didn't tell them why. They thought Jerry and I were going on business and they were just tagging along for some sightseeing. That first night we went to dinner at Hogate's, where we ate so many rum buns that we were almost ready to rehire our personal trainer. Afterward, we attended the National Symphony Orchestra before gathering back at the hotel, where we talked until two in the morning.

The next morning, we were given a tour of the White House and later a tour of the FBI offices, including the shooting range,

> *I was with my mother, who was dying in a Richmond hospital when Jerry and Macel walked into her room.*
> —PATSY CAWTHORNE

where we got to fire Thompson submachine guns. That evening we attended the NRB banquet.

I woke them all up at six the following morning and told them to be in the lobby by seven. They had no idea where they were going when they were whisked away in a limousine. I had tickets for them to attend the National Prayer Breakfast, where President Reagan signed a bill for a Day of Prayer.

When my husband died, Jerry, Macel, Jonathan, and Jerry Jr. all flew to Baton Rouge for his funeral.

—LURLINE BRAUD

My only concern about taking the ladies with us to Washington was that I didn't want any of them to slip up and use my nickname: Mafia Mama. I don't know how the moniker got started, but I'm sure they said it with great affection Still, when you're a pastor's wife and your husband heads an organization called the Moral Majority, "Mafia Mama" isn't the type of title you want floating around Washington.

Shirley's Journey

I had a special bond with each of the women. My bond with Shirley Burton was that she was my traveling companion. I didn't like traveling alone, and when something came up I could count on Shirley. She was a true friend.

It was just after all the ladies had gathered at our cabin on Smith Mountain Lake that Shirley got the news that her breast cancer had returned. While it's always fun to have friends whose good humor make life a joy, it's also a blessing to have friends pull along beside you when life throws you a curveball. That's what we did for Shirley. Though the cancer finally took her life we have never topped missing her smiling face.

We lost two members of our group to cancer, and I didn't want to lose another. Once a year I schedule mammograms for us as a group. With the right attitude you can have fun doing *anything*, including having mammograms. If anyone misses her appointment, I don't rest until it's been rescheduled and I know she's suffered through hers like the rest of us. Fair's fair, after all.

Once, before Shirley died, when she and Bev Lowry were out on a boat on Smith Mountain Lake, Jerry and I snuck into the Lowrys' cabin and took their purses. I'm sure anyone listening could have heard their voices echo across the lake—they thought they'd been robbed.

Practical jokes were one of Jerry's favorite forms of normalcy, and the more he drove through Liberty's campus scaring kids with the air horn on his truck and pretending to run them down, the more we knew that he had survived PTL. Life was back to normal.

CHAPTER NINE

The Later Years

The day began like any other. Jerry sat in his office on the campus of Liberty University meeting with local businessman Daniel Reber, when a phone call alerted him to flip on the television. He watched the replays of late-breaking news in horror. The color drained out of his face as he dialed Dr. Ron Godwin's cell phone.

"Someone just flew a plane into one of the twin towers!" he said, his voice trembling.

Dr. Godwin drove to Jerry's office, where the men watched in stunned disbelief as another airplane flew into the second tower of the World Trade Center. They watched in horror as smoke billowed from the Pentagon and from the crash of a fourth hijacked airplane.

America was under siege.

Stunned by the scope of the unfolding tragedy, Jerry canceled his meetings. Like most Americans he kept a prayerful vigil in front of the television. As the count of the dead continued to rise, Jerry turned to Dr. Godwin, his eyes pools of grief, and said, "How many innocent people died today? How many brave men died trying to help?"

Exhausted from the emotional roller coaster, Jerry scheduled a special chapel meeting to pray for the victims, their families, and the nation. Late that afternoon, the switchboard lit with calls from the media asking for interviews.

"Dr. Falwell did nonstop interviews beginning late in the day on September 11, 2001, and all day September twelfth and thirteenth," Dr. Godwin recalls. "Physically and emotionally exhausted, he rose to the occasion in order to help his hurting country. All of those interviews were with the secular media, asking for Jerry's response to the tragedy.

"On September thirteenth, Pat Robertson's people called and said that Pat wanted to interview Dr. Falwell on the *700 Club*. I moved things around to work it into his schedule. With Pat, Dr. Falwell mentally shifted gears. He wasn't talking to the secular media; he was commiserating with a fellow minister and theologian."

To understand how things went awry that day, you must grasp the biblical perspective of sin and judgment as Jerry did. While most people understand the concept of personal sin, many are not aware of what the Bible teaches about national sin. Israel is a good example of this concept. When God told the Israelites that He was going to give them the land He'd promised (Israel), He told them He was giving them the land not because of their righteousness, but because the national sin of the people living there had risen to such a level that God would allow them to be defeated and dispersed. For instance, in Deuteronomy 9:5 God told Israel, "It is not because of your righteousness or the uprightness of your heart that you go in to possess their land, but because of the wickedness of these nations that the Lord your God drives them out from before you, and that He may fulfill the word which the Lord swore to your fathers, to Abraham, Isaac, and Jacob."

Whenever Israel obeyed God, no army on earth could defeat them. God parted the Red Sea for them. He sent an angel who killed 180,000 of their enemies in one night. But God told the people of Israel that His protection was conditional on their obedience to His law. Although they were God's beloved and chosen people, when their national sin rose to a certain level—and they didn't repent—He withdrew His protection and they were defeated by their enemies and dispersed for hundreds of years. He never forsook them, but He would allow disaster to come upon them to cause them to return to devotion to Him.

This is a simplified version of what the Bible teaches, but suffice it to say that the concept of national sin is what Jerry had on his mind the morning he read about *Roe v. Wade*. He knew that regardless of what the Supreme Court ruled, God considered the killing of millions of innocent babies a grievous national sin. Add to this his concern over prayer and Bibles being removed from schools, and the rising tide of homosexuality, and you can begin to see his alarm. Some theologians who'd studied Bible judgments knew that America's national sin was rising to dangerous levels. Unless people repented, they knew, God would remove His protection from this land.

It was the steady rise in national sin that had prompted Jerry to form the Moral Majority. He understood that repentance and a shift back to God's law would hold back judgment and keep God's protection over the nation. Without it, he knew, our descendants would not long live in a free America.

Jerry was exhausted when he agreed to the interview with Pat Robertson, and never anticipated that Pat would ask him who bore the responsibility for God's removing His protection from America. Jerry answered by defining the sins that were raising the level of national sin: abortions, homosexuality, and other forms of ungodliness. It is probable that Pat Robertson would have answered in exactly the same terms if asked.

The outcry against him was overwhelming. People thought Jerry was blaming the events of September 11 on those who had committed those sins in our nation. Like most ministers in America, Jerry considered himself a citizen of two worlds: God's kingdom and the United States. The *natural* cause of the attacks on the World Trade Center and the Pentagon was terrorists who'd deceived themselves into committing heinous crimes. The *spiritual* reason God had withdrawn His protection from America, thus allowing the attacks at all, was the rising level of national sin.

Later, Jerry wished he had given a different answer. He realized that the true responsibility lay not only with those who were pursuing unrighteous lifestyles but also with the church that had not provided strong enough moral leadership.

God said, "If My people who are called by My name will humble themselves, and pray and seek My face, and turn from their wicked ways, then I will hear from heaven, and will forgive their sin and heal their land" (2 Chronicles 7:14). It was up to Christians to pray and repent for the nation. It was primarily the church's apathy against national sin that had allowed the attack to take place.

Jerry also regretted saying the words he did when he said them. He realized that two days after the terrorist attack wasn't the time to discuss national sin, not on television, even when speaking with a fellow theologian. It was time for the nation to begin the healing process. Theological reflection could come later. Jerry was also grieved that his remarks had added another sorrow to already grieving people.

For all those reasons, Jerry issued an apology.

He received criticism from many theologians who agreed with him and thought he should have stuck to his guns. But Jerry believed that as a nation we needed to stand together in unity against our enemies and not become polarized in our pain.

Regarding the events of September 11, in his apology Jerry said that he would never blame any human being except the terrorists. What he'd been trying to say in the interview was simply that national sin had left us vulnerable to their attack. Jerry was distressed, in part, because this was exactly the type of horror that he and many other ministers had foreseen when the Supreme Court legalized abortion. Jerry knew that it was the great mercy of God that had withheld judgment for years while giving America time to repent and return to the Christian values upon which she had been founded.

Jerry felt hope for America. He knew that God is slow to anger and quick to forgive. He believed with all of his heart that if God's people would pray and repent and do what was necessary to turn this nation back to godliness, that the hand of the Lord would once again defend us against our enemies.

Death Stalks in Silence

The hospital corridor was quiet that evening February 23, 2005. Most of the visitors, like the Falwell family, had said their good nights and left for home, while their loved ones got settled in their hospital beds to read or watch television until they fell asleep. The sound of quiet voices murmured from the nurses' station and the occasional call light dinged for attention. Into this quiet a doctor, just finishing his rounds, strolled down the hall past Jerry's room. Though his mind was on other things, he happened to glance inside. He froze at the sight.

Jerry Falwell was dead.

Bolting into action, he signaled an emergency call as he checked to ascertain that Jerry wasn't breathing. Tilting Jerry's head back, he pumped air into his lungs, forcing his chest to rise and fall. A team of trained medical specialists surrounded Jerry's bed as they attempted to resuscitate him. One nurse pumped emergency medication through a vein while another recorded the time, dosages, and every event as it unfolded. A doctor slipped a tube down Jerry's throat and into his trachea, connecting him to a ventilator, which forced him to breathe.

I hadn't been home from the hospital long when I got a call asking me to return. I trembled all the way back, confused as to what might have happened. Jerry had been admitted to the hospital for respiratory problems, which had turned out to be pneumonia. But he'd been stable and he seemed fine when we left to go home.

Back at the hospital, I stumbled on shaky legs to the intensive care unit. There I saw Jerry lying in the bed, nearly lifeless, while a machine forced air into his lungs. The doctors had resuscitated him, but he was not conscious. His heart rate marched across the screen of a cardiac monitor and tubes crisscrossed his body. His skin was pale, a kind of chalky color. When I spoke to him there was no answering nod, no opening of those twinkling eyes or squeeze from his hand.

He'd been sedated, of course. I sank into a chair and felt the need for a little sedation myself. *Oh, Lord, don't take him home yet!* my heart cried as I kept vigil beside his bed. I rubbed my hand over his fingers to warm them and shuddered at how close I'd come to losing him. *He stopped breathing! What if that doctor hadn't happened by? What if he hadn't glanced up at just the right second as he passed Jerry's door?*

I closed my eyes and thought back over our years together. They'd been good. So good that I couldn't even let myself think about an end to our life together.

Looking Back

My goodness, we're seventy-one now! I leaned my head against the back of the chair while I held Jerry's hand. *How had that happened?* I let my mind wander back to the beginning of our empty nest.

Jerry Jr. had been the first to pack up and move on campus. I smiled as I remembered how Jerry had tried to be brave. But he couldn't blink back the tears that night. Jeannie had moved to the dorm at the beginning of her junior year. Jonathan—*Bless him, Lord*—had lived at home through college. What a great comfort it had been to have him there.

We were in our late forties by the time the children were finishing their education. That was when Jerry had hatched a plan for me to get mine.

Back to School

I'd regretted not getting a college education, but not enough to miss having children. I believed that my life's call was to support Jerry as he accomplished what God asked him to do and to raise our children, creating a happy home where they would thrive and grow into the people God had created them to be. I knew Jerry had to travel in order to fulfill his call, and I wanted the children to have a parent in the home as an anchor in an ever-changing world. So I determined that it would be me.

One evening I walked into the bedroom after being away on a brief trip, and found a stack of papers on the night stand that had not been there when I left. "What's this?" I asked Jerry.

"What?" Jerry asked, acting nonchalant. "Oh . . . those? Those are your enrollment papers. While you were gone, Jeannie and I got you enrolled at Liberty, and Jeannie picked out your classes." He turned back to the television.

"*Jerry!*" I gasped. "What have you done? I'm too old to go to college now! I don't know if I could even pass the classes! And besides, people would make fun of me. I can hear it now, 'Look at the old lady going to class!' "

Jerry shrugged and refused to fight. I thought that meant I'd won, but the following Sunday morning he stood in the pulpit and announced that I had enrolled at Liberty and was about to start classes in the fall.

I wanted to shake him, but what I wanted even more was to slide out of my seat and into the floor. The whole church applauded me, and I'd never felt so much like an imposter. After services I tried to escape, but everyone who saw me stopped to talk about it. "Macel, I'm so proud of you!" "Maybe I'll go back to college one of these days." "You can *do it!*"

I almost sprinted to the car.

At home I wept. "What were you thinking?"

"That it's your turn now," Jerry said with such kindness that I almost forgot to be angry.

"Jerry, I'm too old!"

"Nonsense."

"Mom," Jeannie asked, "would it help if I took a class with you?"

"You'd do that?" I asked with just a twinge of hope. Jeannie had graduated in only three years but was still too young to apply for medical school, so she'd been picking up a few extra classes at Liberty.

I have to admit that I felt awkward walking the halls with a bunch of kids, but I did it. I took one class with Jeannie, two with Jonathan, and one with my niece Kathy, and none of them died of terminal embarrassment from having me there. I hurried from my classes to the library knowing that being married to the founder and chancellor of the university put a pressure on me that none of the other students experienced. It was embarrassing enough to be a college student in my early fifties. I couldn't fail.

I studied hard, determined not to embarrass myself or Jerry. But even so, some of my math classes were . . . challenging. Jeannie had been a whiz at math so I enlisted her help.

"Mom, you'll never learn it if you don't do the work yourself," Jeannie said in her most stern voice.

"Jerry!" I called. *"Make Jeannie help me with my homework!"*

I did buckle down and work hard. In the end I graduated with a 4.0 average, summa cum laude, and in only three years. I was fifty-three years old as I walked across the stage in a cap and gown to receive my degree. Jerry handed it to me before wrapping me in a hug, while Jerry Jr., Jeannie, and Jonathan applauded.

Pass or Fail

After graduation I was offered a position teaching English at Liberty. I accepted the offer and loved the challenge. The only thing I couldn't handle was the idea of failing some students who just weren't making the grade. I invited some boys to our house after class, sat them at the dining room table, and announced, "Now you *will* write your English paper."

"Aw . . . Mrs. Falwell, we can't!"

"Nonsense," I said, sounding like my chancellor husband.

"We don't even know what to write about!"

"Then let's discuss some ideas," I said. "Things you know about and that interest you would be a good place to start." I slipped into the kitchen to pile a plate with brownies while they worked.

If there was a manual on how to accept an in-law, Jerry could have written it. He was the perfect role model.

—SHARI FALWELL

Their finished papers were so good I was ecstatic, and every one of those boys passed the class.

I loved teaching and would still be doing it if Jerry Jr. and his delightful wife, Becki, hadn't given us the greatest gift—our first grandson.

A New Phase

Jerry Falwell III, whom we called Trey, was an adorable baby and a delightful child with his mass of dark curls. I didn't want to miss a moment of this new and wonderful phase of life called grandparenting.

I remembered when Jerry Jr. had been a baby, and how much he'd changed day by day. Back then, I'd quit a job I loved to raise a boy I loved even more. Although Trey wasn't mine to raise, I didn't want to miss a single milestone in his life. I wanted to build a fort with him, read books, play games, and make up stories. I wanted to host tea parties with my grandchildren and push them on swings. So I resigned my teaching position and gave Trey an A+ for every smile.

As more grandchildren came along, our house resounded again with the joyous sound of children. Jerry and I loved every moment of it. Jerry Jr. and Becki added Wesley to our growing family. Jonathan and his wonderful wife, Shari, delighted us with Jonathan Jr. and Jessica. Jeannie's son, Paul, was the only one who loved sports like Jerry. When he was no more than two years old, Paul would crawl into his poppy's lap and watch sports on television for uninterrupted hours.

Both Becki and Shari got pregnant again around the same time. Becki blessed us with beautiful Caroline, with her mother's dark hair and quick smile. Shari and Jonathan were stunned when the Falwell twin gene surfaced again and they gave us the twins, Nicholas and Natalie.

Jerry and I did the same thing with our eight grandchildren that we'd done with our children. Jerry booked out of the office for all of their birthdays, T-ball games, football games, tennis matches,

217

school plays, and recitals. Our immediate family had grown from five to fifteen—almost half the size of Thomas Road Baptist Church when it started.

Bombarding Heaven

Jerry loved being the patriarch of the family. Now, as I sat beside his hospital bed and listened to the rhythmic whir of the respirator, I begged the Lord to give us more time.

> *Jerry was so personable, and he listened to us and valued our opinions. He went to all of our children's activities from tennis matches to Saturday football games, and loved every moment of it.*
>
> *—BECKI FALWELL*

By morning, news of Jerry's hospitalization had reached the press, and we received calls and letters from friends across the nation, among them Ted Kennedy. We were grateful when Larry Flynt heard of Jerry's problems and sent a letter. One of Jerry's political rivals, Jesse Jackson, called Duke Westover, Jerry's assistant, and expressed his concern.

"How's he doing, Duke?" Jesse asked.

"Doc's on a respirator, Jesse," Duke explained.

"You be sure and tell him that I said America's a better place because Jerry Falwell can't talk," Jesse said, signing off with a chuckle and a promise to pray.

Around the world, Jerry's friends—and a good number of his former enemies—prayed for him. All of Thomas Road Baptist

Church hit their knees as well. The throne room of heaven must have been bombarded with prayers.

God heard from heaven and graciously answered our plea. On March 4, Jerry came home to me.

Jerry wasn't what you'd call a compliant patient. He came home ready to tackle the work that had piled up in his absence. Boisterous and full of life, it was hard to imagine that only days before he'd been in intensive care; even more difficult to imagine was what life would have been without him. I shuddered at the thought, and relished seeing him laugh like a kid when he blew the train horn on his truck as he drove across campus.

"Jerry, stop!" I said when students jumped in fright, but trying to rein him in was a battle I'd lost years before. Ours was a ritual: he did something outrageous and I chided him. But my heart wasn't in it, especially after his brush with death. He heard my words, but looked into my eyes and read my heart. *"Don't stop, Jerry,"* it cried. *"Never, never stop."*

Every year since I moved to Richmond to go to medical school, on my birthday Dad, Mom, my brothers, sisters-in-law, aunts, uncles, nieces, and nephews showed up to celebrate. When I started in private practice, at the beginning of each month Mom and Dad phoned to ask my call schedule. At least four or five times a month when I was on call Mom and Dad drove to Richmond and spent the night with Paul so I wouldn't have to leave him with a sitter.

—JEANNIE FALWELL SAVAS

One Campus for Two Ministries

Jerry's health problems had me on edge. *We've been through tough times before,* I reminded myself. After Jerry had resigned from the Moral Majority and survived the PTL scandal, Jerry Jr. graduated from law school and came back to Lynchburg as Jerry's general counsel and administrative assistant.

Jerry had a whole new batch of goals. One of them had been to make the Liberty University campus one of the best in the nation. Another had been to see Liberty debt free and endowed. Meeting the former goal made meeting the latter one a daunting task.

Back in 1997, after Jerry's two forty-day fasts, Liberty's debt had been reduced to $20 million. However, as the enrollment continued to grow each year, the campus had to expand to meet the growing demands for classrooms, dormitories, and dining space.

I left Lynchburg thirteen years ago and got out of the will of God. Doc came after me. "Ron," he said, "you need to come back to where people love you. I need you, and you need to get back into God's work." I'd just been offered a position with a company making a lot more money. I knew when Doc asked me to come back he was doing what he'd made his habit. He collected wounded warriors, people who'd made serious mistakes and bad life choices. Doc brought many of us back. He believed in the God of second chances. I came back, resigned to living the rest of my life alone, but at Thomas Road Baptist Church, I met Carol, a Godly widow. Mine is a story of restoration. Thanks, Doc.

—DR. RON GODWIN

In 2001, Virginia's State Council of Education had approved Liberty's first Ph.D. program. Jerry's dream was coming alive before his eyes. But once again, physical space boundaries were hemming them in.

For years, Jerry had kept his eye on the property adjoining the university. At one time it had been owned by General Electric, which was where my mother had worked almost until her death. Later the property had been bought by Ericsson, a Swedish telecommunications company that made cell phones. Jerry had begun praying for the 888,000-square-foot facility, which sat on 113 acres adjoining the Liberty campus. It would provide much-needed space for expansion.

It would also provide enough space to allow Thomas Road Baptist Church to build a new facility and move onto property adjoining Liberty. Getting the two mega-ministries merged into one location had been a dream in Jerry's heart, but at the time it seemed to be the impossible dream. The replacement cost for the Ericsson factory and land would have been close to $100 million. How could we ever afford that when we hadn't been able to whittle down the $20 million debt that Liberty still carried?

Toward the end of 2002, David Green, a Christian philanthropist who owned the Hobby Lobby chain of craft stores, offered to donate property in the Chicago area for a branch of Liberty. The property was wonderful, so Jerry and the other Liberty leaders studied their options to see what having an out-of-state campus would mean. Eventually they decided that it didn't fit with any of their long-range goals for the university.

Around that time, we heard that Ericsson's corporate headquarters had decided to sell all of its property in North America.

By faith, Jerry believed the property belonged to Thomas Road Baptist Church. The factory would be sold to the highest bidder, and Jerry prayed that the Lord would show him what to bid.

"Bid $10 million," Jerry told Jerry Jr., who represented him in the purchase.

"No, I don't think so," Jerry Jr. said. "I think $8 million will be enough."

"No, son, bid $10.2 million in case someone else offers $10 million even."

If Jerry hadn't upped the bid we wouldn't have won the auction. We got the factory for $10.2 million, and bought the furnishings and surrounding acreage for another $350,000. It was a great deal with only one hitch—the ministry only had about $4 million available to go toward the purchase.

Jerry's banker promised to lend the balance of the money until he could raise it. On February 13, 2003, Jerry flew to Oklahoma City to meet with David Green in person to thank him for offering them the Chicago-based property, and to explain why they weren't going to accept his wonderful offer. During their conversation, Jerry told David that he was buying the Ericsson building located adjacent to Liberty.

In a mind-boggling turn of events, David Green decided that since the building in Illinois wouldn't work for Liberty, he would buy the Ericsson factory for them! Five days later, he wired $10.55 million to Lynchburg. Liberty and Thomas Road Baptist Church began some renovations on the factory and in the following year, 2004, we moved into the space—debt free.

Jerry's last huge goal had been to move Thomas Road Baptist Church onto the property adjacent to Liberty. Every time in the past that he'd tried to borrow money to build a new church facility he'd run up against a stone wall. The project would cost between $30 million and $40 million, and our local bank wouldn't lend us that much. With the donation of the Ericsson facility, the cost for building the church was cut by two-thirds.

Not long after Jerry was released from the hospital, the bank approved the new loan amount. Jerry was as excited as a child at Christmas as he planned his new sanctuary.

Nightmare Night

A few weeks later, on March 28, 2005, Jerry and I spent a quiet evening at home. He sat in his office, the soft glow of a lamp spilling light onto the plans for the new sanctuary that were scattered on his desk. The light cast shadows over the usual golden glow in my cheery kitchen as I wiped down the countertops and the television kept a steady stream of chatter.

"Macel!"

It was Jerry, calling me.

Something in his voice sent chills up my spine. I hurried toward him before he finished the last syllable. "What?"

"Drive me to the hospital!"

My heart did a somersault because I knew Jerry would never ask to go to the hospital unless . . . I didn't want to think about *unless*. "Jerry, let me call nine-one-one!"

"No, I want you to take me." he said, his face a pasty color as he stumbled out the back door and down the steps to the car.

Grabbing my purse and car keys, I followed, still begging him to let me call an ambulance. Climbing into the car seemed to take all his energy and he fell against the seat panting while I sped down the street toward the hospital. My hands were sweaty on the steering wheel, and I felt an overwhelming sense of dread. Something was very wrong, but I had no idea what to do except get him to the hospital as fast as I could.

I managed to keep an eye on the road ahead, shooting through yellow lights and turning corners too fast, while watching Jerry in my peripheral vision.

Oh, Lord, help me! I thought as I sailed through a light. We were only halfway to the hospital when, without warning, Jerry slumped over sideways, his weight pressing against me and his head on my shoulder.

"Jerry?" No answer. *"Jerry!"* I cried, holding his head with my right hand and driving with my left.

He wasn't conscious. Tears streamed down my face while I felt, watched, and listened to see if he was breathing. *Nothing.* Was there a pulse in his neck? I couldn't tell, but even in a state of hysteria I knew one thing without a doubt: my husband, my lover, and my best friend had died.

I screamed, roaring my agony like a wounded animal.

And I drove, speeding, blinded by tears, willing myself to be there. Finally, I saw the lights of the hospital. Several people—staff wearing scrubs—stood out front talking and taking a break. I got my window down and screamed. *"My husband is dead, help me!"*

Without a moment's hesitation they bolted toward the car. They lifted Jerry onto a gurney and rushed him through the automatic doors to the hospital. I climbed out of the car and followed them inside as pain seared through my chest.

Stuck in Quicksand

There's something I'm supposed to do. I pressed my fingers to my temple, trying to think. *Call someone. I'm supposed to call someone. Who?* My mind felt muddled, as though it weren't working on full power.

I followed the gurney and saw them working in a fever trying to resuscitate Jerry. The searing pain across my chest took my breath away. I felt as though I were in a dream in which I was trying to run for help but my legs wouldn't move. I ran, hard and fast, but felt as if I had sunk into quicksand and my feet couldn't find leverage. I was stuck in a nightmare, but the most horrifying part was that I wasn't asleep.

I was awake, and the nightmare scene that unfolded before me was real.

I couldn't remember Jonathan's number, or Jerry Jr.'s, or Jeannie's. I felt as if someone had taken an eraser and wiped the slate of my mind clean. Fumbling through my purse, I found my cell phone and pushed a button that rang through to Dave Randlett, the senior associate pastor at the church.

I then called Jerry Jr. *"Your dad's dead!"* I wailed into the phone.

The next thing I knew one of the nurses wrapped her arm around me. "Are you all right?" she asked, watching me with an experienced eye.

"My chest . . ." I said, rubbing a hand across it to try to ease the tightness there. She whisked me away to another bed in the emergency room and gave me medication.

Fresh Troops

Jerry Jr. and Becki arrived at the hospital about twenty minutes after my call. Jonathan had taken his family out of town. That night around 11:30 p.m., Duke Westover rang him. "Your dad's back in the hospital."

"What's going on?" Jonathan asked.

"I don't know. Your mom called Dave and . . . well . . . she thinks he's dead."

Jonathan called Jeannie and told her he would pick her up on the way home. By 3:30 in the morning the whole family had arrived. They found me in a bed with chest pain and Jerry on a respirator in intensive care. The miracle was that we'd both survived the ordeal.

Doctors explained that while they'd been successful at resuscitating Jerry, he'd been without oxygen for a while before I'd gotten him to the hospital. Only time would tell if he were brain damaged. I felt relieved now that Jeannie, a physician, was at Jerry's bedside.

That weekend was a tough one on the body of Christ. At the Vatican, Pope John Paul II died, in the United States, Billy Graham was in the hospital, and Jerry was on a ventilator.

"Dad was on a ventilator for four days," Jeannie remembers. "From a medical point of view, his having gone into respiratory arrest twice in the space of a month was not a good sign. In addition, there was the valid concern that he'd sustained brain damage while he was without oxygen. We had to wait until he regained consciousness to see how his brain was functioning. Over the next couple of days I saw him open his eyes and look around, but it wasn't purposeful and he didn't recognize anyone. Both of those were signs of brain damage.

"Then one day he opened his eyes and saw Mom. A look of such profound joy crossed his face that I had to fight back tears. I knew at that moment that God had not only spared Dad's life, He'd also protected him from brain damage."

Preparing for Transition

Jerry was discharged on April 6, and we brought him home like a hero returning from war. We enjoyed a few weeks at home before Jerry's doctor sent him for evaluation at the Cleveland Clinic.

"We're going to take you into the cath lab and put three stents into your coronary arteries," the cardiologist explained. "The stents will open the arteries and allow you to have good blood flow to your heart. If we get in there and have any trouble, we'll take you straight into open-heart surgery."

Over the years Jerry Jr. had slaved alongside Jerry on behalf of Liberty University, and Jonathan had done the same thing for Thomas Road Baptist Church. Before going in for the procedure, Jerry named Jerry Jr. vice chancellor of Liberty and Jonathan co-pastor of Thomas Road. He'd spent years preparing both of them for the transition when he could no longer stand at the helm of those great ministries, and he wanted everything in place now that he faced more heart problems.

Jerry breezed through the stent procedure and came home with more energy than I'd seen in him for quite a while.

He Loved Those Kids

Each morning he loved roaming the new construction that was always in progress on Liberty's campus. He watched the new dorms go up like a mother watches over a beloved child. He got back into his habit of attending all of the university's sports events, cheering them on as though they were his kids. And, in a way, they were.

On occasion Jerry would take me shopping and sit in the car and doze while I made my purchases. Almost every time it happened, people passing by tapped on the window while calling, "Are you all right?"

Finally, a friend made a sign that he taped to the window. It read, "I'm not dead. I'm just sleeping while my wife shops." The sign worked, and no one interrupted his nap.

Kathy Rusk, Jerry's assistant for seventeen years, saw how he related to people at the office. "We had thousands of students on campus," Kathy explains, "and most of the time when their family visited, they always wanted to introduce them to Dr. Falwell. In all the years I worked for him, I never saw him turn anyone away. No matter how

> *Unlike many pastors of large churches, Jerry wanted to stay connected with his congregation, and one way he did that was by making his own hospital visits. Until he went home to be with the Lord, he made hospital visits several times a week, and he would perform anyone's wedding or funeral who asked, if he could fit it into his schedule. Sometimes I sat beside him at a Liberty baseball game and he'd say, "Mark, see that guy up at bat? His sister just found out she has cancer." He loved those kids.*
>
> —MARK DEMOSS,
> EXECUTIVE ASSISTANT

busy he was, if a student's family wanted to meet with him, he stopped whatever he was doing to talk to them. On occasion, when he was working against a tight deadline, he might ask them to come back later, but he never turned them away.

"Another thing I noticed over the years was that if one of his grandchildren wandered into his office during a meeting, the meeting stopped long enough for him to give them attention. He always made sure his family knew that they were of utmost importance to him. His grandchildren would play on his computer while he was out of the office and change his screensaver, but it didn't bother him. He laughed every time it happened.

"More than once I walked into his office and found Trey on Jerry's computer, and Dr. Falwell working in a chair with his papers in his lap. He didn't just tolerate the interruption—he loved it, and would sigh with contentment. In all the years I worked for him I never saw him angry. He didn't believe that there was any reason to hurt anyone's feelings."

Fifty Years

The following year, 2006, got off to a difficult start when my sister Mary Ann died on January 26. Although she'd never married or had children of her own, Mary Ann played a significant role in the lives of her nieces and nephews. They adored her.

That year also saw the realization of several of Jerry's goals. First, on February 13, the American Bar Association approved provisional accreditation for the Liberty University School of Law. At the time, there were only 193 accredited law schools in the

> *Jerry never let himself get removed from the people. When we
> traveled to other places for him to speak, the pastor would often
> pick us up for service and say, "Jerry, after you preach, I'll have one
> of my associates close in prayer so that we can slip out for dinner.
> "No, I don't want to do that," Jerry always said. "I want to stay and
> visit as long as the people want to talk to me." Sometimes that
> meant that we didn't get home until two in the morning, but he loved
> people. He was never a big shot, which was remarkable given the
> size and scope of his ministry.*
>
> —MARK DEMOSS

country, and getting provisional accreditation on the first try was
deemed impossible.

In addition, construction was under way for the new sanctuary
of Thomas Road Baptist Church, to be located on Liberty Mountain. Jerry had designed the sanctuary, which featured 6,000 theater seats, a wrap-around balcony, and a massive choir loft. The
52-by-410-foot lobby had already been dubbed "Main Street," and
would accommodate seating areas, displays, and an indoor playground for children.

Jerry's goal was to have the new sanctuary finished so that
Thomas Road could move to its new location on the day we celebrated our fiftieth anniversary: July 2, 2006.

"There's no way," the contractor said, shaking his head in
dismay.

Jerry took it over the man's head. You might say that he took
the matter to a Higher Power. Against all odds, the new sanctuary
was finished in time for our fiftieth anniversary celebration.

Had it really been fifty years? Fifty years since thirty-five of us had gathered in the old Donald Duck Bottling Company. Fifty years since Jerry had knelt in that little sanctuary and pictured it filled with people, thousands of people. Fifty years since God had given Jerry the vision to take his city for Christ. Thousands of people had heard the Gospel from the pulpit, over radio, or on television. Jerry had knocked on thousands of doors and shared the good news face to face.

I'd been playing the piano for church services since I was a teen at Park Avenue Baptist Church. Fifty years earlier, I'd played for our very first service, and I'd been playing at Thomas Road Baptist Church ever since. I thought our move to the new location was a great time for me to pass the baton and move on through the rites of passage. After fifty years, I resigned as pianist.

Baseball Cards

Moving Thomas Road Baptist Church to Liberty Mountain had been Jerry's last major goal. There were other things he'd wanted to do, but he'd fought a good fight and there were no more giants to kill, no more wars to win, only the occasional skirmish. Thank heaven that he had eight grandchildren whom he adored.

Jeannie's son, Paul, had a habit of coming up with something he wanted for Christmas that just couldn't be found. That year, two weeks before Christmas, nine-year-old Paul asked the Santa at the mall for a Mickey Mantle baseball card.

"I'll do my best, Paul," Santa said, "but I'm not sure about the baseball card. Those are pretty hard to come by."

"At least I didn't ask for a Honus Wagner card!" Paul said in defense.

Who in the world is Honus Wagner? Jeannie thought, but didn't ask. Instead she picked up the phone and called Jerry.

"Dad, Paul has asked for a Mickey Mantle baseball card for Christmas!"

"Well, at least he didn't ask for Honus Wagner," Jerry said with relief. "Honus Wagner," he explained, "is the most costly baseball card in existence."

"I'm *so* glad he didn't ask for Honus," Jeannie replied. "Can you help me find a Mickey Mantle?"

"I'll do my best," Jerry said, excited at the prospect. For the next two weeks he called Jeannie every morning with a status report on his search. On December 23, he almost jumped for joy.

"I've got the card!" he told Jeannie. "I'm going to FedEx it to you now so that Paul will have it when he wakes up Christmas morning."

Jerry had already left to go to FedEx when the phone rang again. "Mom, stop Dad," Jeannie said. "I think it would be better for Dad to give Paul the card in person when we get to Lynchburg."

I don't know who was more excited about the Mickey Mantle card that Christmas, Paul or Jerry.

A few months later, in April 2007, Jerry phoned Jeannie, quivering with excitement. "I've got something else for Paul!" he announced. "I found a display of twenty-five Mickey Mantle cards!"

When Jeannie and Paul came home for Easter, Paul saw the display of Mickey Mantle cards and lit up like a Christmas tree.

Later he said, "Mom, Poppy gave me these Mickey Mantle cards and it wasn't even my birthday. Why didn't he wait?"

"I don't know, Paul," Jeannie said, pondering the question herself.

Heaven on His Mind

I f you read someday that Jerry Falwell has died," Jerry said over the years, "be assured that I was greatly surprised. I've asked God for another fifteen years with the option to renew."

During our Easter service in 2007, Jerry said something that sent a chill wind through my soul. "God's man is invincible until he finishes the job God gave him to do."

That spring, heaven seemed to be on Jerry's mind more than it ever had been before. During chapel one morning he said, "When I die, there's a song I want sung at my funeral. It was written by Don Wyrtzen, and the name of it is 'Finally Home.' "

Tears streamed down Jerry's face and his voice choked when he talked about waking up in heaven and finding himself finally home.

More and more often Jerry would stop a meeting with Godwin and other staff members and say, "let's talk about what God has done." Together they'd have a little praise-fest, mentioning all the miracles God had performed and all the answered prayers. Lifting his face and praising God, the atmosphere

> *If you read someday that Jerry Falwell has died, be assured that I was greatly surprised. I've asked God for another fifteen years with the option to renew.*
>
> —JERRY FALWELL

filled with glory and it seemed as though heaven came down to earth.

Spring flew by and in the second week of May, Jerry preached his last chapel service of the semester. That morning Jerry Jr.'s car broke down and he was late getting to work.

"Aw, you missed the *last* chapel!" Jerry said when he arrived.

Jerry Jr. froze, looking at his father's face. *He doesn't think he's going to be here next semester.*

CHAPTER TEN

Living Legacy

A quiet murmur of conversation hummed through O'Charley's as I finished the last of my steak soup and hot bread. Our waitress, who had just become the latest in a long line of recipients of full scholarships to Liberty University, hovered nearby in case there was the slightest thing we needed.

Jerry still hadn't eaten his food. He'd spent the evening memorizing my face as though he didn't already know every smile line and wrinkle.

I'd taken my time over my meal and allowed myself a side order of memories for dessert. What an adventure I'd embarked on the moment I put my hand in Jerry's and whispered the words *I do*.

I'd do it all over again. I chuckled, and Jerry raised an eyebrow. If I'd known back then what our lives would entail, I might have run. But even after fifty years of ups and downs, knowing the good times and the tough ones, I would do it again. That, I figured, was part of the legacy my husband would one day leave behind.

I wasn't alone in these sentiments. All the people who'd worked to help him build Thomas Road Baptist Church, all those who'd helped pioneer Liberty University, all those who'd fought alongside him for the Moral Majority, and even all those who'd stood by him in the PTL scandal—we would do it all over again.

"Are you finished?" Jerry asked when I pushed my plate aside. He helped me out of the booth and drove us home. We talked in hushed tones long into the night.

An Ordinary Day

The next morning, May 15, 2007, Jerry started his day as usual. He began with prayer, and then at 7:00 a.m. he phoned Ron Godwin to confirm their breakfast meeting at Bob Evans Restaurant. When it was time to leave, he gave me a kiss and a smile and said, "I'll see you later."

The hostess at Bob Evans ushered Jerry and Ron to their usual table and they ordered their usual breakfasts. As was his habit, Ron had prepared two typed lists: one list of problems and one list of opportunities. "Ron, you handle the problems list," Jerry said, handing it back over. "Now, let's talk about the opportunities."

They worked their way through everything on the list, brainstorming, planning, and looking at all the angles until Jerry was satisfied.

"Okay," Jerry said, a look of joy on his face, "now let's go over what the Lord has done!"

As the two men rejoiced in the Lord, Jerry was as upbeat and cheerful as ever. But Ron thought he seemed tired. Jerry had undergone some medical tests over the past two weeks, but Ron wasn't satisfied.

"Listen, Doc," Ron said, "why don't we fly to Cleveland and let them check you out?"

"No," Jerry said, "if there's something wrong they wouldn't do another stent, they'd probably do real surgery, and we've got to get through commencement and graduation. Come on, let's go get some work done. We have a television meeting at eleven."

After their breakfast Ron drove to his office on the north campus and Jerry drove to his office at the old mansion on the grounds, which served as an office building for the university.

No Answer

A while later I called Jerry's cell phone. No answer. That wasn't unusual. Sometimes he forgot to turn it back on after a meeting.

But a chill rippled up my spine and I *knew*. I knew it in the same way that I'd known President Reagan had been shot. I knew it in the same way that I'd known the birth order of our children.

But I didn't want to know.

I took a deep breath. I wanted this to be a normal day. I wanted Jerry to be in a meeting with his phone turned off. I dropped into a chair and pushed the irrational knowing aside.

I called Jerry's assistant at the mansion. "Kathy, Jerry's not answering his cell phone. Is he in his office?"

"No, Mrs. Falwell, I haven't seen him yet this morning."

I couldn't let it rest. Something was wrong—worse than wrong. I called Kathy two or three times that morning. Jerry still wasn't answering his cell phone. Kathy still hadn't seen him. I told Kathy to see if Jerry's car was in the garage. I shut my eyes and tried to still my pounding heart. *No, Lord. Please no.*

At 11:00 Kathy got another call, this time from someone on the church staff: "Dr. Falwell didn't show up for his meeting in the television department. Is he coming?"

A sick feeling settled in the pit of Kathy's stomach. She'd worked for Thomas Road Baptist Church for thirty years, and she'd been Jerry's assistant for seventeen years. She'd never known him to miss a meeting. Kathy called Jerry Jr. to let him know that his dad was nowhere to be found. Jerry Jr. called Randy Smith, LU's police chief and told him to search the campus.

Kathy then opened the door to the garage and saw Jerry's car parked there. *Maybe he passed out in his car,* she thought, peering inside. Nothing. She quickly called Jerry Jr. again. Jerry Jr. told Randy Smith to rush to the mansion office.

If Jerry had gotten sick in his office she didn't want to embarrass him, so Kathy sent Mark Smith to check. Mark hurried to Jerry's office and found the door shut and locked. He could hear Jerry's cell phone ringing inside.

Meanwhile, I called Jonathan in his office. "Your dad's *missing!*" I wailed.

"Missing? How could he be missing? He probably just forgot to turn his cell phone back on. I'll find him and have him call you right away."

A Flat Line

Jonathan then called Kathy. She cryptically answered, "Jonathan, you need to come over here."

What she didn't say was more terrifying than what she said. Jonathan left the building in a dead run. Two minutes later he raced into Jerry's office, the scene forever burned into his memory. Jerry lay on the floor, while two of Liberty's police officers performed CPR. Jonathan dropped to his knees and grabbed one of Jerry's lifeless hands.

"Dad, we still need you! *Please!* We're not ready to let you go!"

Tears streaming down his face, Jonathan turned to Kathy. "Call my brother. Tell him to pick up Mom and meet us at the hospital. Get Jeannie to the hospital. Have one of the staff drive to the school and get my brother's and my children and bring them to the hospital." Turning back to his father, he prayed.

Ron Godwin then arrived and rested his hand on Jonathan's shoulder, the look in his eyes stark with grief. Emergency medical personnel arrived, starting an IV and giving Jerry cardiac stimulants, but the flat line on the cardiac monitor didn't change.

Shari, Jonathan's wife, rang his cell phone. Unable to speak, Jonathan struggled for words. Finally, "Dad's not breathing. Meet us at the hospital."

Jonathan glanced outside when they were getting ready to transport Jerry to the ambulance. A crowd had gathered, and a local television station was filming. "Move them back!" Jonathan called to the police. Jerry might have been a public figure, but everyone should have some dignity in death.

When the ambulance screamed into the emergency room drive, Jonathan asked them to shield Jerry by using an ambulance to block the view from the press that had gathered in the parking lot. Inside, more than twenty medical staff stood in silent tribute to the man who'd made hospital visits several times a week for fifty years, who'd preached to them, encouraged them, and loved them.

When I arrived I found Jonathan holding Jerry's hand, alternately praying and pleading, as teams of people worked at a furious pace to try to revive him. A nurse helped me into a chair beside the heartrending scene. I watched, tears streaming down my face, as they worked to resuscitate him. It had worked twice before, I reminded myself. It could work again. I wanted it to work again. I wanted him to wake up and beam with joy to see me.

But deep inside, I knew it wouldn't happen.

I knew it before anyone realized he was missing. I knew it before anyone broke down his door or started CPR. And still a flame of hope leapt to life when Jerry's doctor rushed in and asked permission to take him to the cath lab and try a procedure that might save him. Hope is a wonderful thing.

Unrelenting Pain

Becki, Shari, Jonathan, Jerry Jr., Jeannie, and I waited in a tiny office while they worked in the cath lab. Jonathan pulled up CNN news on the computer. The headline read, Falwell Dead. He turned off the machine and waited for the doctor to tell us what we already knew.

Finally he came and told us. The procedure had failed. Jerry was dead.

Knowing it didn't make hearing it any easier. It didn't ease the feeling that a part of me had been amputated when I walked into the home we'd shared for so many years and Jerry wasn't there. It didn't ease the agony each time I reached across the bed and found it empty. It didn't stop the ache caused by his too quiet office, the chair he would never sit in again, the papers he would never shuffle to straighten. It didn't help when I sat alone at the breakfast table without him reading the morning paper cr drinking his coffee.

There were a million losses that it did not help, but occasionally between waves of sorrow that threatened to knock me down and wash me away in their undertow, it did help. It helped because the *knowing* had been God's way of assuring me that Jerry was with Him. Jerry had stepped on that shore and found it heaven. He'd touched a hand and found it God's. He'd breathed new air and found it celestial. He'd woken up in glory and found it home.

It's clear to all of us now that Jerry had known he was going home. That's why he'd memorized my face at O'Charley's the night before. That's why he'd been so disappointed that Jerry Jr. had missed chapel five days earlier: Jerry had *known* it would be his last one. That's why he'd given Paul the display of Mickey Mantle cards in April instead of on his birthday: he'd known he couldn't wait for a special occasion. He died a month later.

That's why he'd stood in chapel and wept over the thought of heaven: his heart was already there.

A Final Good-bye

I, of course, was not in heaven. I felt like I was coming apart at the emotional seams from the loss of him. It wasn't just me; the whole family was adrift at the thought of navigating through life without him. He was such a vital part of all our lives. Jerry Jr. and Jonathan had worked with him every day for years, and Jerry had spoken to Jeannie almost daily. Yet somehow we made the decisions that had to be made.

Jerry lay in repose at the Arthur S. DeMoss Learning Center at Liberty University. Thousands of people came to pay their respects. When it came time to transport his casket to Thomas Road Baptist Church for his funeral service, we wanted a horse-drawn hearse. Becki made calls among the Amish and found just what we wanted. Pulled by two black horses, it was a black wooden hearse with windows through which you could see the casket. Thousands of people lined both sides of the road as the horses pulled Jerry's casket for one last tour of Liberty University.

The sanctuary was filled for his funeral. Many of Jerry's friends spoke in the service: Dr. Jerry Vines, Dr. Franklin Graham, Duke Westover, Dr. Jim Moon, Dr. Harold Willmington, Dr. Ron Godwin, Dr. Elmer Towns, and our daughter, Dr. Jeannie Savas. Tim Goeglein addressed the crowd on behalf of President Bush.

I hadn't known that Jeannie was going to speak, but she did a beautiful job of reminding everyone that Jerry had completed what God called him to do. She urged people not to expect Jerry Jr. and Jonathan to fill their father's shoes, because they have to fulfill their own call in taking both Thomas Road and Liberty on from here.

Included in the music for the service was the song Jerry had requested, "Finally Home."

After the funeral procession circled Liberty Mountain on its way to the grave site just outside of Jerry's mansion offices, they drove past the old homestead where Carey and Helen had raised their children. They drove up to Candler's Mountain, where he'd played as a child. And they wound their way through 5,000 acres of the Liberty campus, to finally come to rest before the church he'd loved and served for fifty-one years.

> *What I will miss most are his prayers. Dad used to call and tell me what he was praying for me, but even when he didn't tell me, I knew he was praying. I could literally feel his prayers.*
>
> —JEANNIE FALWELL SAVAS

Surviving Without Him

The days following Jerry's funeral passed in a blur of agony for me. But somehow I remembered the young waitress from O'Charley's. I called to set up her scholarship, and at this writing she was a student at Liberty. Jerry would have had it no other way.

We received an avalanche of mail from people whom Jerry had helped over the years, many of them including stories I'd never heard before.

I heard from President George W. Bush soon after Jerry died, and the following day President George H. W. Bush phoned to give his condolences. "What can I do for you, Macel?" he asked.

"Before he died," I said, "Jerry promised all our grandchildren a trip to the Oval Office."

"Fine," President Bush said, "I'll let you know the date. Is there anything else?"

"My grandson Paul is sitting here and he's never spoken to a president."

"Put him on!"

The two of them had a great conversation. Before long, President Bush's office called back with a date for us to visit.

We all arrived on the appointed day and were ushered into the Oval Office, where the president spent forty-five minutes visiting with us and having his picture taken with each of the children. He also gave each child a gift bag.

Leaving a Legacy

What a legacy to be so respected by the president of the United States that he would take the time to comfort our mourning family. Yet, if Jerry were here today, he would say that the greatest legacy of his life was his children and grandchildren who will carry the message of Christ to the next generation.

He also left a legacy in Liberty University, the largest evangelical Christian university in the nation. Liberty University, sprawling over 5,000 acres in the Blue Ridge Mountains, offers a top-rank faculty, a progressive academics program, cutting-edge technology, and all NCAA sports—as well as 35 miles of mountain bike trails, and an ice arena. With a current enrollment of 10,500 students, Liberty is training young champions for Christ from all 50 states and 80 foreign countries.

In the last nine years of his life, Jerry and his staff doubled Liberty's residential enrollment, tripled its square footage, and

> *Dad wanted to be remembered as a husband, father, grandfather, and a pastor, but he was Superman to me. He was always my hero.*
>
> —JONATHAN FALWELL, PASTOR, THOMAS ROAD BAPTIST CHURCH

paid off millions of dollars in debt. Even in death, Jerry had planned ahead: his life insurance paid off all of Liberty's debt and started an endowment.

Jerry left a legacy in the form of Thomas Road Baptist Church, which had grown from a seedling of thirty-five members in an old bottling company to a church of more than 21,000. In the first eight months following Jerry's death, Thomas Road Baptist Church celebrated with 2,700 who gave their hearts to the Lord Jesus and 1,700 new members who were added to the church.

Jerry was a visionary. His vision for Thomas Road Baptist Church couldn't be contained in the Donald Duck Bottling Company any more than it could be contained in Lynchburg. With a hunger to reach those who'd never heard that Jesus paid the price for our sins, the ministries of Thomas Road Baptist Church have reached far from Lynchburg to help hurting people around the world.

Jerry left a hard-won legacy to this nation. He had opened the door for conservatives, including Christian conservatives, to have a voice in government. In the process, he created what is called the Religious Right. He offered a fearless example of how to be a citizen of *both* worlds—the kingdom of God and this earth. Through the Moral Majority, Jerry helped catapult Ronald Reagan into the White House. Many historians have credited President Reagan with the collapse of the Communist bloc of the former Soviet Union. That is a legacy which President Reagan left to the world, and one in which Jerry played a part.

In stepping into the PTL fracas, Jerry made a bold stand against sin and immorality in the body of Christ. He refused to turn a blind eye to corruption, and set a standard of righteousness for all Christians to follow.

Yet perhaps the crowning achievement of all these, the ultimate legacy of Jerry Falwell, was that he refused to let anything stand between him and his family.

A Life Well Lived

Who was Jerry Falwell? He was, at heart, a pastor, and it was that heart that motivated everything he did. He was pastor to his young family, with a reverence before God that most families find lacking. He fought for families, his own and others. He was pastor to Thomas Road Baptist Church. He was pastor to the young people who walked the halls of Liberty University. It was his pastor's heart that led him to fight the political process on behalf of Christians everywhere.

Jerry Falwell left behind a life well lived.

While I appreciated the legacy, I loved the man even more. After Jerry's death I had a burning desire to know if there had

---

The day before he died, Dad dropped by my office and said, "Go with me up to the monogram on Liberty Mountain." I was swamped with work and couldn't afford the time. "I just don't have time today, Dad." Then I saw the look on his face. It was rare to see him so disappointed. "You know, on second thought, I would love to go." We sat up on top of the mountain and talked to Liberty University students. It was one of Dad's last gifts to me, and I will always cherish the memory.

—JERRY FALWELL JR.

been anything we could have done—a follow-up visit to the Cleveland Clinic, open-heart surgery, anything—that would have lengthened his life. I approved an autopsy to get those answers.

We were amazed to learn that all three of Jerry's stents were still in place and the arteries were still open. His cholesterol was normal, and he'd never had a heart attack. The doctors believe he died from a cardiac arrhythmia.

Piecing together a timeline, it appeared that Jerry had left his breakfast meeting with Ron Godwin, driven to his office, and parked his car in his private garage and entered his office via a rear entrance without speaking to anyone in the building. Sometime that morning he'd walked across his office and stepped out of this life into another.

Last Words

I believe that Jerry died much the same way he lived. He walked to the edge of eternity, turned backward onto the balls of his feet, and, with his arms splayed out and a smile on his face, he fell into the arms of his loving Father.

It was that quick and that simple. I know there was a crowd gathered for his homecoming. Among those who met him were his parents—Carey, whose face Jerry hadn't seen since he was fifteen years old; and Helen, his beloved mother; his brother Lewis; and sisters, Rosha and Virginia. I know that my mother, father, and sister Mary Ann joined the celebration. What a family reunion it must have been.

During Jerry's funeral, Jeannie described the hospital scene in

2005 when Jerry had been unconscious and was feared brain-dead. She told how when he'd opened his eyes and seen my face, unabashed joy radiated from his. Jeannie said she believes that he'll have the same look the first time he sees my face in heaven.

I believe that, too. Which is why—although we mourn—we do not mourn as those who have no hope.

The night before Jerry died, Harold Knowles, who had been his friend for fifty-five years, had a dream. At 7:00 a.m. the following morning, while Jerry was making arrangements with Ron Godwin for breakfast, Harold described the dream to his wife.

"I dreamed that I took Jerry to a train station where he was leaving on a trip. He wore suit pants, a dress shirt, and suspenders, and his coat was slung over his shoulder. Just as he was boarding the train, he turned to me and lifted his red Bible."

" 'I'll see you later!' he called."

Strange, I realized later: those were the last words he spoke to me.

I'll see you later.

Yes, Jerry, because of the blood of Jesus shed on Calvary, because of the empty tomb and the precious promises of God's Word, and because of your faithfulness to preach the Gospel around the world, you will greet a multitude of us one day.

We will indeed . . . see you later.

A Final Farewell from

Jerry's Grandchildren

Poppy always introduced me proudly as "Jerry Falwell the Third," even though everyone else calls me Trey. Also he would require me to tell everyone I met that I was "Number One."

I would often sneak out of high school during lunchtime and go eat with him. My favorite thing to do with him was to drive around Liberty campus and see all the progressing construction sites. He would thoroughly describe the site enough for me to create a mental image of the finished project. As we drove around, he would aim his black GMC at students walking on the sidewalk and blow his ear-piercing train horn as we both laughed at how the students jumped scared to death.

He attended almost every football game and tennis match in which I was involved. Five days before he died, he was there to watch me win the tennis conference championship in singles. Although he had to leave early for a graduation, he called my dad every several minutes to get an update on the match. After the match he called me to tell me how proud of me he was for winning the championship, which meant the world to me. Poppy always told me not to ask for anything I didn't want because he would make sure I got it.

Poppy was my hero.

Jerry Falwell III
Age 18

Poppy was always upbeat and cheerful. He was full of energy and had a positive outlook on the world. Whenever he saw me, he always reminded me how much potential I had in life. He said that he could tell I would end up being a preacher or a lawyer. He always introduced me as Charles Wesley Falwell because he was proud of the fact that I have the same name as a famous preacher.

It was obvious that Poppy loved us all very much. I was glad he heard my brother, Trey, and me play the drums and the guitar in the basement a few weeks before he died. We had spent about a year and a half learning how to play and he never would have heard us if he hadn't come by that day.

Wesley Falwell
Age 14

I miss my grandfather so much. He was so nice to me. He loved me so much. I miss the way he called us "kookiebirds" and how he tickled us all the time. Before he died, the many times he was in the hospital, we were all so scared and thought that was his last day. At least we got to spend a couple more years with him. He would always come and scare us wherever we were. I loved him for that and many more reasons.

He would always buy gifts for us and I was very grateful. We would always watch TV together in the "Rock Room." I would spend the night at their house as much as I could. He and I would always go to the Liberty games like football, basketball, and baseball. In fact, about a week before he passed away we were at a baseball game. I was downstairs in the batting cage with my cousin Briana. When Poppy came downstairs when the game was over, I showed off for him by hitting a few balls. That was only part of the last week.

The last week before he died was awesome. I can remember Michael W. Smith playing a concert. We were in the back room listening. Poppy introduced me to him. After that we drove around town. Poppy got Grandmother some jewelry. While we were driving around town, Jessica and I were listening to the Michael W. Smith CD. We went to the college place for students who were married. We were driving around town and we saw a bear. We went to bed, and a couple days later it happened.

During the school day, I did every thing a normal kid would do in school. Then we got picked up from school. And we were taken to my dad's office. Then we were taken to the hospital and found out everything. He died. We were very sad. We stayed away from school for awhile and my classmates sent me notes.

I miss him so much. I still can't believe that he's gone. We've been taking care of Grandmother though, and I know he'd be happy about that. I know one thing for sure. Even though I still can't see him, I know he's there with me all the time.

Jonathan Falwell Jr.

Age 11

I still miss him and love him. I know that he used to call us kookie-birds. The last time I saw him, he called me a nutcase. Whenever we would go to a restaurant, he would come in and kiss us upside down on our heads while we were sitting in our chairs. I miss him and still cry sometimes but I know he is in heaven looking down on us right now. I loved my Poppy so much and nobody will ever replace him.

My grandmother is still upset about us losing Poppy but she is the same though. She still has lots of time to play with us. Sometimes she dances with me in my room. My brothers and sister and me take turns staying with my grandmother so she's not alone. It's lots of fun. She is a little bit different without Poppy but I still love her very much.

Jessica Falwell

Age 10

I'm Paul, and I liked all the same things my Poppy did. We both liked sports a lot. Poppy came all the way to Richmond to watch the Super Bowl with me. I also went down to the "Rock Room" with him to watch football, baseball, or basketball whenever we were in Lynchburg. I always asked him which team we where cheering for unless Liberty or LCA was playing.

He took my cousin Trey and me to a New York Yankees game against the Orioles. The Yankees won! He also took Trey, Wesley, and me to a Washington Redskins game against the New York Giants. The Redskins won! He taught me how to throw a spiral in my backyard. We both liked the same foods, too. We were the only ones to eat fruitcake and drink eggnog during Christmas.

One time I was with him and we went to go see these LU students at Camp Hydaway and he blew his hornblaster and scared everybody to death. Before he got his hornblaster, he had this video that showed these people scaring people with the hornblaster. Poppy loved playing jokes on people.

My grandmother taught me how to play flashlight tag. She plays board games with me when I ask her to, and she goes bowling with me sometimes. When I go to her house we walk around the circle with her and play with her big dogs. She loves to read us stories, too. It is really fun when I go to her house.

Paul Savas
Age 10

Poppy gave me a big hug every time I saw him and told me how pretty he thought I was. He always came to my birthday parties and school plays. On my seventh birthday (April 27, 2007), he came out where my friends were swimming and made us all laugh. He was fun.

I loved him and miss him very much.

Caroline Falwell
Age 7

My Poppy was a very funny man. He always made me laugh. He would tickle us and make funny faces at us. He would also grab us and play with us a lot when he would sit in the chair in our house. He called us kookiebirds. He also scared us a lot, which was funny sometimes, but sometimes it made me mad because it would really scare me. I really miss him a lot. I look at pictures of him in my house all the time and we have a bobblehead of him on our fireplace. I'll never forget him.

Natalie Falwell
Age 7

My Poppy was a great man. I love my Poppy. I miss him very much. He always acted silly around us kids. He'd make funny faces and really funny noises and he would always try to scare us. His favorite toy was his car horn and it scared me sometimes, but most of the time it was just annoying. He always tried to make us smile and it worked. It's quiet now without him and kind of sad, but I know when I see him in heaven, he'll tickle me and make me laugh again.

Nicholas Falwell
Age 7